Realizing Community

'Community' is so overused both in everyday language as well as in scholarly work that it could easily be dismissed as a truism. However, the persistence of the term itself shows that the idea continues to resonate powerfully in our daily lives, ethnographic accounts as well as theoretical analyses. This book returns a timely and concerted anthropological gaze to community as part of a broader consideration of contemporary circumstances of social affiliation and solidarity.

Over the last twenty years, community *as an idea* has overtaken community *as social interaction* in a number of influential works. However, without elucidating the actual social relations in which the idea of community is realized, it is difficult to account for the emotions it calls forth. Thus, while the essays in this book acknowledge the conceptual, imagined dimension of the construction of communities, they also seek to re-embed their accounts of community in a social context.

The chapters cover a whole gamut of ethnographic cases from small localities, regional identities, transnationally dispersed personal networks to more limited and ephemeral relationships. The authors contribute invigorating new material to an established and crucial area of anthropological study.

European Association of Social Anthropologists

Series Facilitators: Jon P. Mitchell, University of Sussex and
Sarah Pink, University of Loughborough

The European Association of Social Anthropologists (EASA) was inaugurated in January 1989, in response to a widely felt need for a professional association that would represent social anthropologists in Europe and foster co-operation and interchange in teaching and research. The Series brings together the work of the Association's members in a series of edited volumes which originate from and expand upon the biennial EASA Conference.

Titles in the series are:

Realizing Community

Concepts, social relationships and sentiments

Edited by Vered Amit

London and New York

First published 2002
by Routledge
11 New Fetter Lane, London EC4P 4EE

Simultaneously published in the USA and Canada
by Routledge
29 West 35th Street, New York, NY 10001

Routledge is an imprint of the Taylor & Francis Group

Typeset in Galliard by
M Rules
Printed and bound in Great Britain by
TJ International Ltd, Padstow, Cornwall

British Library Cataloguing in Publication Data
A catalogue record for this book is available from the
British Library

Library of Congress Cataloging in Publication Data
Realizing community: concepts, social relationships and
sentiments / edited by Vered Amit.
    p. cm – (European Association of Social Anthropologists)
Includes bibliographical references and index.
1. Community – Congresses. 2. Social interaction –
Congresses. I. Amit, Vered, 1955– II. European Association
of Social Anthropologists (Series)

HM756 .R4 2002
307 – dc21   2001048404

ISBN 0 415 22907 3 (hbk)
ISBN 0 415 22908 1 (pbk)

Contents

Acknowledgements

I would like to thank Jon Mitchell for his thoughtful guidance and many helpful suggestions both for this project as well as for a previous volume (*Constructing the Field*) in the EASA series which I also edited. I would also like to thank the audience of anthropologists who participated in the session of the EASA (European Association of Social Anthropologists) conference, Frankfurt, 1998 from which this volume derived. The comments and feedback provided by members of this audience as well as their encouragement for the compilation of this volume were a crucial element in bringing this manuscript to publication.

Contributors

Vered Amit is an Associate Professor in the Department of Sociology and Anthropology at Concordia University, Montreal. She has conducted fieldwork in London (UK), Quebec and Grand Cayman. She is currently conducting research on transnational consultancy. Among her previous publications are *Armenians in London: The Management of Social Boundaries* (1989) and *Constructing the Field* (2000). She is currently editing a *Biographical Dictionary of Anthropology* and is collaborating on a project with Nigel Rapport entitled *The Trouble with Community: Anthropological Reflections on Movement, Identity and Collectivity*.

Anthony P. Cohen is Provost and Dean, Faculty Group of Law and Social Sciences, University of Edinburgh. He is the author or editor of ten books including *The Symbolic Construction of Community* (1985) and most recently *Signifying Identities: Anthropological Perspectives on Boundaries and Contested Values* (2000). He has conducted fieldwork in Newfoundland, Canada and the Shetland Islands, Scotland.

Andrew Dawson is lecturer in social anthropology at the University of Hull. His books include *After Writing Culture: Epistemology and Praxis in Contemporary Anthropology* (1997) and *Migrants of Identity: Perceptions of Home in a World of Movement* (1998). His principal interests are in post-industrial society and refugee experiences. He has worked in England, Eire and Northern Ireland, and is currently undertaking work on displaced Bosnians in Australia, England and former Yugoslavia.

Noel Dyck is Professor of Social Anthropology at Simon Fraser University in British Columbia. He has studied relations between Aboriginal peoples and governments since the 1970s and is the author of *What is the Indian 'Problem'?: Tutelage and Resistance in*

Canadian Indian Administration (1991). His current research focuses upon adult involvement in the organization of children's sports as well as the nexus between immigration, integration and sport. He is the editor of *Games, Sports and Cultures* (2000).

John Gray is currently Reader in the Department of Anthropology, Adelaide University in Australia. He has two sites of continuing ethnographic fieldwork – a multi-caste village in the Kathmandu Valley, Nepal and a sheep farming locality in the Scottish Borders, each leading to the publication of a monograph: *The Householder's World: Purity, Power and Dominance in a Nepali Village* (1995) and *At Home in the Hills: Sense of Place in the Scottish Borders* (2000).

Signe Howell is Professor of Social Anthropology at the University of Oslo. She received her D.Phil at Oxford based on her work on religious ideas and practices among an aboriginal group of people in Malaysia: *Society and Cosmos: Chewong of Peninsular Malaysia* (1984, 1989). She has subsequently conducted research among a group of people in Eastern Indonesia: *For the Sake of Our Future: Sacrificing in Eastern Indonesia* (1996) before becoming engaged in her current project on transnational adoption.

Marian Kempny is Docent (Associate Professor) at the Institute of Philosophy and Sociology, Polish Academy of Sciences, Warsaw. He has just completed two research projects on globalization, tradition and locality interrelations based on fieldwork carried out in selected local communities in Poland. Recent publications based on these studies include: 'Managing Locality among Cieszyn Silesians in Poland', in *Roots and Rituals: Managing Ethnicity*, (eds) T. Decker, J. Helsloot and C. Wijers, Amsterdam 2000; 'Local identities as an issue under the conditions of globalization', *Globalization and Identities*, ed. Paul Kennedy and Nadeem Hai, vol. I, Manchester Metropolitan University 1999, pp. 1–13. 'Nationale Identitaet und Staatsburgerschaft im postkommunistischen Polen', in *Kulturelle Identitaet und sozialer Wandel in Osteuropa: das Beispiel* Polen (Beitraege zur Osteuropaforschung, Band 3), Z. Krasnodębski, K. Staedtke and S. Garsztecki (eds), Hamburg 1999, pp. 195–206. He has also published extensively on anthropological theory and history: *Anthropology without Dogmas, Social Theory without Illusions*, Warsaw 1994 (in Polish).

Karen Fog Olwig is a Senior Lecturer at the Institute of Anthropology, University of Copenhagen. She has conducted extensive research on the development of African–Caribbean culture, focusing on the cultural construction of place and community. She is currently conducting research on global family networks resulting from migration. Her publications include *Global Culture, Island Identity: Continuity and Change in the Afro-Caribbean Community of Nevis* (1993) and *Siting Culture: The Shifting Anthropological Object*, edited with Kirsten Hastrup (1997)

Nigel Rapport is Professor of Anthropological and Philosophical Studies at the University of St Andrews. He has carried out fieldwork in England, Newfoundland and Israel. His most recent books are *Transcendent Individual: Towards a Literary and Liberal Anthropology* (1997), and *Migrants of Identity: Perceptions of Home in a World of Movement* (1998). Currently, he is collaborating with Vered Amit on a project entitled *The Trouble with Community: Anthropological Reflections on Movement, Identity and Collectivity.* (forthcoming).

Chapter 1

Reconceptualizing community[1]

Vered Amit

It is difficult to discern much in the way of coherence among the multitude of definitions, descriptions and claims of community which occur in quotidian conversation as well as within a variety of scholarly work. Some fifty years ago, efforts to manage this cacophony analytically through competing definitions of community dominated the field of community studies, consigning it 'for some time into an abyss of theoretical sterility' (Cohen, 1985: 38). In 1955, G. A. Hillery was able to list numerous definitions of community which had by then appeared in the sociological literature, an inventory cited in more recent work as an illustration of the futility of such taxonomic approaches (ibid.; Lustiger-Thaler, 1994: 21; Baumann, 1996: 14), even of the dubious analytic utility of the concept of community altogether (Cohen, 1985 and this volume, Baumann, 1996: 14). So why, at this juncture, should we return our attention and analyses to such an ostensibly hackneyed term?

For one thing, the sheer proliferation of its invocations provides a backhanded testament to the continued popular saliency of this concept. Even the commonly inane or cynical everyday plays on this term suggest a connotation sufficiently 'compelling' (Cohen, Epilogue to this volume) that it can be called upon to imbue the banal with second-hand poignancy. This begs an obvious, but unresolved question: what is it about this idea and/or form of sociality that continues to so engage our attention? It is difficult to see how sociologists and anthropologists could easily ignore such an intriguing issue. Indeed, however much they may have bemoaned its sloppy manifestations, they have never entirely ceased their efforts to address it. And in spite of the fact that these efforts have not succeeded in producing analytical precision, they have, notwithstanding the multiplication of definitions, featured a remarkably sustained focus around a few key questions. From scholars such as Tönnies,

Durkheim and Weber writing at the turn of the twentieth century (Chorney, 1990) to the urban studies of the Chicago School in the first half of the twentieth century (Hannerz, 1980; Park, 1925; Wirth, 1938), to the later responses of Oscar Lewis (1965) or Young and Willmott (1957/1962) and the more recent work of Anthony P. Cohen (1982, 1985), Benedict Anderson (1983/1991) and Gupta and Ferguson (1992), to name but a few, social analysts have repeatedly used the concept of community as a vehicle for interrogating the dialectic between historical social transformations and social cohesion. While they frequently offered conflicting responses, these scholars shared a preoccupation with the implications of capitalist evolution, state formation, urbanization, industrialization and later globalization for the principles, conceptualizations and logistics of social affiliation. In short, community has been a long-standing, although by no means an exclusive, conceptual medium for interrogations of the interaction between modernity and social solidarity. Far from sidelining this preoccupation, recent changes in the nation-state form, patterns of mobility, communications, technology and transnational connections have surely spotlighted it even further.

From social relations to social imagination

The tendency for an analytical focus on community to be linked with issues of 'modernization' is certainly apparent in the history of anthropology. In the work of such early scholars as E. E. Evans-Pritchard (1940) or Margaret Mead (1930/1942), terms such as 'society', 'culture' or 'peoples' appeared with far greater frequency than 'community'. Community appears to have obtained greater analytical prominence when anthropologists began to shift their research to cities, where the populations they studied were incorporated into state systems and when they began to interrogate more self-consciously the limits of their field of inquiry; in short, when they converged on to the terrain of complex societies they had hitherto consigned to sociologists. In these circumstances, community resonated as a limited subunit, inextricably but also problematically embedded in wider social and cultural contexts, the antithesis therefore to antecedent characterizations of 'primitive societies' as unitary isolates. There have, however, been important distinctions in the way in which anthropologists have interpreted this embedded quality.

In an essay on 'the production of locality', Arjun Appadurai (1996) distinguishes between locality and neighborhood. He defines locality as primarily relational and contextual, a phenomenological aspect of social life, categorical rather than either scalar or spatial. Neighborhood, on the other hand, he defines as actually existing social forms in which locality is realized: 'Neighborhoods, in this usage, are situated communities characterized by their actuality, whether spatial or virtual, and their potential for social reproduction' (Appadurai, 1996: 179). In this volume, we are concerned with a wide range of collectivities, including some forms which would not normally be apprehended under either of Appadurai's terms. But the general distinction he is drawing between category and phenomenology *vis à vis* actual social relations is apposite. Indeed, I want to argue that the conceptualization of community in anthropological and related literatures has involved a marked shift away from community as an actualized social form to an emphasis on community as an idea or quality of sociality. In turn, this thrust towards ideation has been associated with a translation of community as collective identity rather than interaction. It is useful at this point to review several key works that can serve as historical signposts for these transitions.

During the 1950s and 1960s, the studies conducted by anthropologists from the Rhodes-Livingston Institute and the University of Manchester in the Copperbelt towns of southern Africa marked a concerted early venture by anthropologists into urban locales (Hannerz, 1980) and with it an effort to consider the construction and contextualization of new forms of urban community. In Luanshya, A. L. Epstein (1958) and J. Clyde Mitchell (1956) outlined the emergence of new forms of urban association and categories amidst a diverse and newly constituted population of African labor migrants (drawn from a variety of rural locales), European managers, miners and colonial administrators. Tribal identities did not disappear in this urban environment, but increasingly pertained to classifications rather than the realized corporate groups they constituted in rural areas; tribal distinctions were superseded by the dominant biopolitical cleavage between Europeans and Africans; tribal elders were displaced by the urban leadership of new organizations like the miners' trade union and the African National Congress. The urban community was identified with the social system of the town (or rather two towns since Epstein argued Luanshya consisted of two separate units: the mine compound and the municipal location), this developing, complex and diverse constellation of relationships, organizations and conflicts. Community and categorical identities were thus clearly distinguished, the latter operating as constituent rather than overruling elements in the structure of social relations comprising the town. The Copperbelt researchers were aware of the need to relate this urban locale to its broader social context and concerned to distinguish their approach from other community studies which had been criticized for a failure to address external influences (Hannerz, 1980: 145; Epstein, 1964). Significantly, Epstein (1964) related this need for contextualization to a reflexive consideration of the ethnographer's role in constituting the limits of his field of study. There is much in this body of research which resonates with contemporary concerns: a focus on the construction of place (Olwig and Hastrup, 1997), the production of local subjects (Appadurai, 1996: 185); the relationship between locale and context (ibid.: 184); and the role of the ethnographer in delimiting his/her field of study (Amit, 2000). Nevertheless, this treatment of urban locale/community as a tenuously articulated and emergent field of political relations was rapidly overtaken by a return to an older more *Gemeinschaft*-like version of social solidarity.

Thus, a flurry of anthropological and sociological studies published during the 1960s (e.g. Lewis, 1965; Gans, 1962), themselves developed in reaction against a preceding negative portrait of urbanism as social disorganization, stressed the persistence of 'folk' relations of intimacy – kinship ties, religious participation, informal systems of support – in local, face-to-face urban neighborhoods. It was this older, resurrected inflection of closeness and familiarity which was taken up in two later works that did much to inscribe a reading of community as a 'structure of feeling' (Appadurai, 1996: 199) and identification increasingly detached from actual social relations. Accordingly, when Arjun Appadurai argues that late twentieth-century orientations towards deterritorialization and displacement have created a disjuncture between 'neighborhoods as social formations and locality as a property of social life' (ibid.), one can only note that we have already visited this theoretical ground before when it was used to account for rather less novel processes of state formation and urbanization. It behoves us therefore to consider the outcome of this vision rather than simply to revisit it uncritically.

Anthony Cohen's 1980s work on community, belonging and boundary reflected the interpretative turn within the anthropology of the period. He was concerned with the meanings people attribute to community and their membership in it. When focused selectively on British rural localities, of which Whalsay, his long term ethnographic base, was an exemplar, Cohen appeared to have in mind a thick version of community, an intricate structure of relations and ways of belonging. In these milieus, people knew a good deal about each other and engaged with each other not in terms of specialized roles, but rather as 'whole persons'. But since this personal knowledge of individuals could become quite easily converted into public knowledge, people had to adjust their behavior accordingly, being careful about what they revealed:

> They have to accord with the conventions of intimate society and, at the same time, they have to resist the tensions inherent in the too-close coexistence of small-scale society. With the accumulated folk knowledge of tradition and of their own lifetimes people adjust to each other to produce and maintain order and coherence. If such a community is to survive in its valued form, its structure must be organised accordingly, and a strict regimen recognised and accepted for its maintenance.
>
> (Cohen, 1982: 11)

These communities were distinctive cultural entities but, drawing on Barth's (1969) previous theory of ethnic boundaries, Cohen argued that people became aware of this culture when they stood at its boundaries and, further, that this awareness of difference crucially informed their attachment to locality (1982: 3). Ethnicity and locality were thus homologous, they were 'both expressions of culture' and of collective identities (ibid.). Indeed, culture and identity were treated as inseparable because people think of culture in terms of their local identities. Albeit the interpretive orientation of Cohen's analysis, in many ways his initial account of community was much closer to the earlier classical anthropological versions of society and culture than to the much more fragmented portrait of urban locality which appeared in the Copperbelt studies. Community was not simply locale; like the small-scale societies of the earliest ethnographies, it had become the nexus of an inextricable convergence between culture, place, intricate social relations and collective identity. Community was thus converted into a form of 'peoplehood' that was now very deliberately and self-consciously inserted into complex societies. This was not an isolated and self-contained form of peoplehood, but a fundamentally relational one.

When Cohen attempted to extend his model of community beyond the rural localities that had inspired it, he maintained the emphasis on identity and relationality, but stripped the term of its more particular substantive components (Baumann, 1996: 14). In his much cited 1985 essay, community had become less a matter of social practice and institutions than a symbolic framework for thinking about and conveying cultural difference.

> Our argument has been, then, that whether or not its structural boundaries remain intact the reality of community lies in its

members' perception of the vitality of its culture. People construct community symbolically, making it a resource and repository of meaning, and a referent of their identity.

(1985: 118)

Community had thereby become much more than locality, for now it could be extended to virtually any form of collective cultural consciousness. By the same token it had also become much less, since it was no longer necessarily an effect of the social relations and institutions which had been such a crucial constituent of British rural communities like Whalsay or less cohesively of Luanshya, an urban community in northeast Rhodesia. It is this attenuation of community, its levitation as an idea, a symbol for collective identity mediated by individual subjectivity that assumed such primacy in later examinations of community in anthropology and cultural studies. But nonetheless, it was clear that for Cohen, even in this stripped-down version, community was still most real the closer one got to the kind of local face-to-face relations that characterized a Shetland island locality (1985: 13).

The linkage between community and face-to-face social relations that was still a feature of Cohen's exposition was unabashedly severed in another influential theorization of community published in much the same period. Benedict Anderson(1983/1991) appropriated the idea of community as a vehicle for explaining the affective loyalties invested in nationalism. Anderson argued that the rise of print capitalism in the sixteenth century eventually provided the vehicle for a sense of commonality and mutual identification to develop among large dispersed populations. As books became more available and newssheets proliferated, people dispersed across vast spans could come to see themselves as sharing identities and lifestyles. In consequence, the development of nationalism relied on the capacity of a multitude of people who would never meet each other face to face, or even know of each other personally, to nonetheless imagine themselves through the mediation of mass printing as part of the same community. Anderson argued that one should not read 'imagined' as 'spurious' or 'invented', for any community that extended beyond the immediately face to face incorporates this element of imagined commonality. The affective charge of nationalism, the capacity of people to identify with and sometimes even be willing to fight for or die on behalf of strangers crucially drew on a conception rather than actualization of solidarity. Thus, Anderson's work deliberately decoupled the idea of community from an actual base of interaction, or to use Appadurai's terms, posited a fundamental disjuncture between locality and neighborhood and pushed this process backward to a historical crossroad predating current globalization trends by several centuries.

Of course, Anderson recognized that the technologically mediated capacity to imagine likeness was not enough in itself to delimit the boundaries of the national community. After all, in the twenty-first century more advanced electronic forms of communication allow us to imagine even more vividly and immediately our similarities with diverse multitudes of people world-wide. Yet neither our capacity to recognize such semblances nor the efforts of political elites to use these forms of communication to promote particular national allegiances are necessarily or always sufficient grounds for the formation and perpetuation of successful nationalist movements or identifications. Anderson identified such factors as the spatial distribution of print vernaculars, the role of the intelligentsia, state administrative structures, educational systems and other such institutions as manipulating the limits of the imagined community of the nation. But as Michael Herzfeld (1997) has noted, Anderson was not able to provide another piece of the puzzle: the source of the emotional impact of nationalism, the reason that people are sometimes willing to sacrifice themselves for it. 'Why should people be willing to die for a formal abstraction?', Herzfeld wondered (1997: 6). Anderson's theory of imagined community was not able to answer this question, Herzfeld has suggested, because:

> He does not ground his account in the details of everyday life – symbolism, commensality, family and friendship – that would make it convincing for each specific case or that might call for the recognition of the cultural specificity of each nationalism.
>
> (ibid.)

Anderson's top-down approach to nationalism 'says, in effect, that ordinary people have no impact on the form of their local nationalism: they are only followers' (ibid.).

In contrast, Herzfeld used the concept of 'cultural intimacy' to highlight the interplay between official and social discourses, the daily performances, expressions of skepticism, invocations of stereotypes, the uses of irony and humor as means of cultural critique and collective self-deprecation which subtly subvert official discourses of nation, state bureaucracies and citizenship. Yet at the same time, by invoking the 'inside' nature of these activities, these allusions can reinforce and reify the very categories they seem to mock. The process of subversion through day-to-day 'social poetics' thus transforms abstract categories of nationhood into intimate expressions of felt solidarities. In turn, we can use Herzfeld's notion of cultural intimacy to amplify Benedict Anderson's key premise. If communities must be imagined, then by the same token, what is imagined can only be truly felt and claimed by its potential members if they are able to realize it socially, in their relations and familiarity with some, if not every other constituent. To treat the idea and actualization of community as if these are in essence independent elements is to leave us and our analyses with only one hand clapping.

Thus, the sense of community among the Norwegian parents of transnationally adopted children who are the focus of Signe Howell's chapter appears, at first glance, to be an exemplar of a conceptual category without social content. These adoptive families can be found throughout Norway, in urban as well as rural areas. Their children originate from a number of different countries: South Korea, Columbia, China, Russia, other Eastern European countries and Ethiopia. With some 16,000 transnational adoptees now integrated into these dispersed Norwegian families, the majority of their parents will never know each other personally, let alone meet face to face. The only thing they appear to have in common is their shared experience of childlessness and of adopting a child outside Norway. While a strong sense of empathy appears to exist between these adoptive parents regardless of personal relationship, Howell argues that this strong emotional feeling of relatedness would not have come about had they not engaged in face-to-face relationships with other parents at various stages of the adoption process. Adopting parents meet each other in preparatory courses; when they travel together to collect their children; through subsequent get-togethers sponsored by a number of associations; or on the collective return visits to their child's country of origin organized by the adoption agencies. No adoptive parent meets or knows every other such parent in Norway, but the sense of shared experience and connection arises out of ongoing social relations and frequent encounters between particular sets of parents.

It was not, however, this kind of social mobilization, but an insistence on the idea of community as integral to itself that appears to have so excited the social scientists who responded with enthusiasm to Anderson's concept of imagined communities. It wasn't long before imagined communities of one kind or another were popping up almost everywhere. Indeed, nearly a decade later when one arrived at Akhil Gupta's and James Ferguson's application of this notion (1992), the actuality of community seemed a rather vulgar proposition beside the possibilities of an unfettered, imagined version. Anthropologists who had always prided themselves on the attention they paid to the interactions comprising small-scale social groupings now appeared to be far more interested in less literal, and more portable, categorical identities. This excitement appears to have been prompted by the introduction of the concept of imagined communities at a particularly apt intellectual and historical juncture.

For anthropology, the idea arrived at the tail end of an interpretive turn in which, as exemplified by the work of such scholars as Clifford Geertz (1973), an emphasis was placed less on social institutions and practice than on the reading of these by particular actors. Ethnography thus became a textual exercise in search of meaning rather than a science of observation in search of verifiable data. This interest in interpretation overlapped with a period of disciplinary introspection and critique during the late 1980s (Marcus and Fischer, 1986; Clifford and Marcus, 1986) in which an older ethnographic tradition was charged with exoticism and reification even as it, too, was thereby reified. Ethnographers were accused of ascribing social integrity to ethnographic portraits they had uncritically contrived, distorting the positioning of small-scale groupings within wider relations of power and ignoring their own role in crafting ethnographic subjects. Within this melange of auto-critique and interpretation, the concept of imagined community seems to have provided a particularly useful hermeneutic alternative since, by definition, it was concerned with interpretations and ideologies of solidarity rather than contentious social description or, for that matter, social relations. As anthropologists entered the last decade of the twentieth century and took up the popular and scholarly preoccupation with globalization, diasporas, deterritorialization and transnational fields, face-to-face relations seemed to dissolve even further into less tangible 'structures of feeling', of belonging, of imagined community.

Reinserting the social back into community

In a contemporary world in which the local and immediate is often perceived as receding in favor of a flow of people, objects, signs and symbols chasing each other around the globe (Lash and Urry, 1994), it is not surprising that a concept of imagined community would prove so compelling. Yet a simplistic and unidimensional endorsement of this concept as an emblem for high modernity may run the risk of resurrecting a form of cultural determinism even in the midst of celebrating contingency and deconstruction. If community is read as peoplehood and peoplehood is treated as independent of actual ongoing social relations, a construct simply in and of itself, then it is difficult to see how we can avoid two implied choices. On the one hand, we might attribute intentionality to proclamations of community, but, given their lack of social grounding, would be effectively obliged to take these as exercises of greater or lesser cynicism, strategic manipulations of fear or nostalgia. Or, on the other hand, we are forced to treat community as a primordial attachment, an essentialist category of identity that can persist and retain feeling and import even when emptied of social content. Either option robs most individuals of agency, rendering the appearance of proclaimed, desired or intuited collective commonality and sociality – the sense of or will towards community – as instances solely of unselfconscious subjection respectively to demagoguery or mythology. And it leaves us with a tautological argument in which our own inability to account for these instances is explained away by attributing the deficiency of our constructs to the motivations of others. If, however, we are not willing to disavow the analytical challenges posed by the conceptualization and formation of contemporary collectivities, then we have to re-embed community in a social as well as conceptual context.

Anthony P. Cohen (1985) and more recently Arjun Appadurai (1996) have argued that the symbolic or conceptual elaboration of community/locality has become more important in response to a weakening of structural boundaries. As the integrity of local neighborhoods is assailed by state policies or globalizing forces, communality increasingly has to be asserted or imagined symbolically rather than structurally. It is an argument so apparently well suited to contemporary circumstances that it has sometimes been treated as a taken-for-granted assumption in recent anthropological analyses. Yet, there is, after all, something rather odd about our tendency to posit that a notion like community, so redolent with sociality is being invoked ever more frequently as a move *away from*, rather than *towards* social mobilization. Commonsense observation suggests that it is more credible to view proclamations of community as first and foremost claims of, and for, social engagement, whether as recognition of an existing set of social relations or as a call for the formation of new sets of social relations. These are statements in the order of 'we have something in common as a result of our social interaction' or 'we have something in common that can become the basis for future social interaction'. Existing collectivities cannot always be reproduced, and efforts to mobilize new ones can fail, but the imagination of community is always fundamentally oriented towards the mobilization of social relations. Yet while the category invoked and social relations mobilized in the name of community are always linked, they are nev. wholly commensurable and are frequently in tension with one another.

The chapter by Karen Fog Olwig provides an apt illustration of the strain between abstract generalized categories of diaspora and the historically specific, particular and often highly personal social collectivities which are attributed to them. In tracing the dispersed descendent networks of three couples born on the West Indian islands of Jamaica, Dominica and Nevis, Karen Fog Olwig avoided designating them *a priori* in terms of such general categories as 'Caribbean', 'diasporic' or 'migrants'. Instead, she used the vehicle of life-history narratives to elicit the kinds of 'communities of belonging and sentiment within which they inscribe themselves from their particular social, economic, geographic and personal vantage point'. Edwin and Henry, respectively members of the Nevisian and Jamaican family networks, had both settled in Britain and experienced fairly similar occupational histories and material success, but they had established themselves in very different kinds of local communities and expressed very different senses of Caribbeanness. Olwig argues that Edwin's and Henry's respective experiences of migrating and settling in Great Britain had been influenced by their disparate backgrounds in the Caribbean but had also been mediated by the global fields of family relations in which they continued to participate. The lifestories of Edwin and Henry were part of ongoing conversations within their widely dispersed family networks. Like Howell, Olwig therefore emphasizes the ongoing and interpersonal, if not always face-to-face, social relations through which individuals interpret generalized categories such as Nevisian, Jamaican or English: 'Individuals therefore did not just imagine their place, cultural identity or home in the Caribbean, they also experienced them through concrete and intimate relations with family members, and the narrative communities that they constituted' (Olwig, Chapter 7).

It is through this kind of interplay and incongruity between the actualization and categorization of community that the capacity for an ironic appreciation of such connections is rendered not simply possible but unavoidable. Nigel Rapport (Chapter 8) defines irony as an appreciation of the 'malleability and the mutability of all social rules and realities, and the contingency and ambiguity of cultural truths'. Rapport notes that a number of commentators have attributed the development of ironic detachment to particular historical and cultural developments: the impact of technological change, science, particular literary traditions, or of modernity more broadly. In contrast, Rapport argues that the cognitive processes involved in ironic detachment are universal. Everywhere and at every period, human beings have been able to detach themselves sufficiently to question the value and rationale of conventional practices and truths and to imagine alternatives.

Indeed, if human beings did not have this capacity for detachment, it is difficult to see how they could ever contend with the numerous inconsistencies of even the most stable everyday situations, the inevitable changes imposed by the life cycle as well as equally inevitable, if less predictable, social changes. If ironic detachment is integral to social and cultural process generally, it is by the same logic an indispensable element in the construction of community, a claim that is implicitly acknowledged in the well-entrenched anthropological emphasis (Cohen, 1985; Barth, 1969) on the relational character of community and social identity (i.e. that these are always constructed in respect to the possibility of alternative allegiances or identifications). It is therefore not difficult to see why sociological questions about community have so often been linked with the interrogation of systemic social changes which create or require alternative forms of social solidarities. But if we accept that irony is a universal aspect of social process, then we need to reorient accordingly the questions we pose about the dialectic between community and change. Just as ironic detachment is not a capacity peculiar to a particular period of history, so too the salient question of community is not, as the early Chicago School urbanists contended, whether it can exist in one kind of social system rather than another (Hannerz, 1980; Cohen, 1985), for the impetus towards social connection and commonality is as universal as our ability to regard these skeptically. Rather, what is at issue in the interaction between change and communities are the ways in which the construction or deconstruction of the latter provides a means for people to apprehend and locate themselves within a world that never stands still. In one way or another, the accounts of community in most of the chapters in this book are accounts of creative engagement with social and personal changes.

During the 1980s, the people of Teviothead, a parish and electoral district in the Scottish borders region that formed the focus of John Gray's study (Chapter 3), felt that their local community was declining. The decline was assessed in terms of a dwindling population and in the diminished state of three core institutions: school, kirk and community hall. Meanwhile, the uniform and particular nature of hill sheep farming which was central to the Teviothead sense of community was changing as a result of the European Community's Sheep Meat Regime. Farms now became diversified between, on the one hand, breeding farms that continued to sell pure-bred hill lambs identified with specific farms, shepherds and borders hill sheep farming and, on the other, commercial farms which raised fat lambs to satisfy anonymous, European Community-wide certification standards. Nevertheless, people in Teviothead continue to maintain a sense of place through the practices of 'hefting on' and selective breeding in which hill sheep, particularly tups (rams), come to embody and mediate homologous consubstantial relations between a family and its farm. In turn, the kula-like circulation of highly valued tups through sales at the Lockerbie auction serves to constitute a clique of eminent breeders whose farms collectively define the larger locality of hill sheep farming. Lesser tups are also sold to commercial farms, creating a shared sense of attachment between 'hill sheep farming people, inclusive of both breeders and commercial farmers, and the border region'. If Teviothead has declined as a community, its residents, in common with other farmers throughout the Scottish borders, appear to be improvising a regional sense of community mediated by hill sheep.

Marian Kempny's chapter is also concerned with processes of place making in this case in a region that has been subjected to a succession of political and social regimes. Cieszyn Silesia is a border region nowadays divided between Poland and the Czech Republic. Traditionally, religious distinctions between Lutherans and Catholics constituted the main source of differentiation among the diverse population of this region. When the territory as a whole was controlled first by the Bohemian Crown and then by the Habsburgs of Austria, this religious source of differentiation overlapped with national and linguistic distinctions. Yet in reverse to the pattern in the rest of Poland, in this region it was Lutherans who spoke and viewed themselves as Poles, while Catholics tended to speak Czech and to be viewed as strangers. When, at the end of World War I, the region was partitioned into Polish and Czech parts, and when, in the eyes of the Polish Catholic Church and most Poles, Lutheranism was equated with Germanic identity, Lutherans retreated to their confessional communities. A strong link between religious identity and place was heightened by the tendency of Catholics and Lutherans to occupy separate parishes. But socialist industrialization and urbanization after World War II restricted public expression of religion and brought a massive influx of new Catholic inhabitants into this area which served to erode the distinctions between Catholics and Lutherans and to encourage a sense of ecumenical localism instead. This localism has not receded even in the face of further dramatic political and economic changes after 1989 which, among other developments, lifted religious restrictions. Instead, there has been a renewed and pervasive emphasis on the distinct regional identity of Cieszyn Silesia (even though it has been incorporated since 1975 into a larger Polish administrative structure) as well as on its pre-partition historical boundaries even though these have for some time been intersected by the borders of two separate states. Religious distinctions continue to be important, but are superseded by the now more significant distinction between established residents and newcomers. Localism, envisaged in historical and transnational terms and expressed in social practices and institutional sites, is forging a new unity of Cieszyn Silesians and a sense of continuity in the midst of turbulent changes.

Ashington, in the northeast of England, once the 'biggest coalmining village in the world', is now facing the closure of its last mine, no alternative sources of employment and a rapidly aging population. In his chapter, Andrew Dawson focuses on the expanding population of elderly people in Ashington and their participation in a proliferating number of leisure clubs catering to this segment of the population. Most of these leisure clubs are designed specifically for the elderly and are run by elderly participants. Handicrafts, sketches, dances, songs and poetry form an important aspect of club life and center around a celebration of community which explores ideas of sameness and difference. Difference is drawn through a contrast between urban, industrial, working-class Ashington and the rural, agricultural and increasingly middle-class surrounding areas. Sameness is represented in terms of shared regional oppression, but most especially as generational. The elderly share and exchange talk about the bodily experience of aging and the common interests and activities this entails. Their shared community-mindedness is also contrasted with the putative selfishness of the young. For these elderly residents of Ashington, community, Dawson argues, is both a cultural resource with which to conceptualize the bodily experience of aging as well as an idea and practice that arises from that experience.

The experience and emotion of community

One could as well extend a version of Dawson's conclusions to the Scottish border and Cieszyn Silesia regions described by Gray and Kempny respectively, where community also appears to have served as a resource with which to conceptualize and respond to change. But it would be a mistake to view these as simply strategic responses or instrumental efforts at social location in the midst of imposed or inescapable change. The sense of attachment and place expressed by elderly people in Ashington, Scottish hill farmers or Cieszyn Silesians provides a resource with which to encounter a changing world precisely because these are felt, embodied and 'emplaced' connections arising out of shared experiences, relationships, histories, territories and practices. It is this sense of complex and sometimes ambivalent mutuality which allows people to perceive themselves as experiencing political, economic and life-cycle changes *together*, an engagement and a position which, in turn, provides ground for reconceptualizing the basis of community.

But a sense of community does not only arise out of historically entrenched, ongoing relationships. The affinities expressed by adoptive parents in Norway or community sports participants in a British Columbian suburb (Dyck, Chapter 6) reflect newly formed relationships between people who would probably not otherwise know each other had they not participated in a common activity. The suburbs of the Lower Mainland of British Columbia have experienced rapid growth and equally rapid turnovers of population. Catering to a transient population, many of whom spend a considerable amount of daily time commuting to and from paid employment, the spatial and social structure of the suburb is not conducive to easy or immediate sociability. Yet, suburban residents do seek to find arrangements for overcoming social isolation and connecting with others. One of these vehicles is participation in an 'organized group', such as the numerous local sports clubs and leagues which at one time or another enlist as many as 50 percent of all children and youth residing in the suburban area studied by Noel Dyck. The participation of children in these activities is made possible by the willingness of parents to serve as volunteer chauffeurs, spectators, chaperones, coaches, administrators and referees. In the course of serving in these roles, parents can find themselves spending considerable time with other parents with whom they may feel they have more or less in common. They may, indeed, alter the nature of their participation in order to limit their interaction with some parents and increase, instead, the time they spend with others. But according to Dyck:

> What needs to be underscored is the manner in which parental involvement in community sports for children not only serves to support the individual and shared project of child rearing but may also facilitate the creation and maintenance of extra-familial relationships and activities for both children and parents, links and events that may also evoke a sense of affiliation and community among participants.

Sustained engagement in their children's sports activities allows parents to move from simply being contemporaries to consociation, but these consociate relationships are not all-encompassing. They tend to be enacted within a diverse field of sporting events and only occasionally extend into other domains. Situationally limited, ephemeral, these relationships nonetheless facilitate the development of a much appreciated sense of belonging.

The modes of community described by Howell and Dyck (Chapters 5 and 6) are newly formed, episodic and partial, but it would be a mistake to conclude that they therefore necessarily constitute shallow and less deeply felt attachments than the affinities entailed in Caribbean family networks (Olwig, Chapter 7), Ciesyn Silesia (Kempny, Chapter 4) and Scottish border hill regions (Gray, Chapter 3) or the shared experience of aging in a declining English mining town (Dawson, Chapter 2). The communities described by Howell and Dyck have developed around the profound sentiments, anxieties and hopes of childlessness and parenting, experiences which are no less emotionally charged and collectively constructed than aging, family, consubstantial relation with land or a sense of a long shared history. Partiality and episodicity are not synonymous with triviality and superficiality, and, as Dyck notes, community need not be all-encompassing or directive to provide satisfying forms of social connection and belonging. Indeed, however much they may differ in terms of historical depth, the range of activities they comprise or their duration, none of the communities described in this volume are all-encompassing. In all these cases, they organize and express only some of the attachments, activities and identities in which their participants are engaged. None therefore constitute the 'terminal identities' once ascribed by A. L. Epstein to ethnicity (1978). We could argue therefore that the relational character of community is as likely to be derived from the multiple attachments of its members as from contrasts with collectivities in which they are not members.

Conclusions

In closing this Introduction, I would like to highlight the implications of several key insights furnished by the chapters in this volume. First, all of these case studies illustrate the visceral nature of community, that these are not coldly calculated contracts, but embodied, sensual and emotionally charged affiliations. The sense of belonging and attachments described in this volume are, at one and the same time, experienced as highly personal and collective. This is not always comfortable, but it is rarely trivial. But then we are hardly original in emphasizing the emotive character of community. Indeed, one of the most constant elements in a century of sociological attention to the changing nature of social solidarity has been consideration of this element of affect, whether viewed as diminishing in the shift from one kind of social association to another (Wirth, 1938) or attributed as the impetus for broad social mobilizations (Anderson, 1983/1991). However, this previous scholarly representation of the affect of communality has tended to feature two extreme positions that have rendered 'true' community as either exceptional or inexplicable.

On the one hand, we have been offered a *Gemeinschaft* version in which the emotive charge of community arises out of multiplex, longstanding interpersonal relationships of deep intimacy and familiarity. Here community is thick and entire. This representation of community was a key feature of late nineteenth- and early twentieth-century sociological accounts of a nostalgic pre-industrial European past, but, as I noted earlier in this chapter, it has frequently resurfaced in one form or another in later analyses. Since, in an increasingly complex and mobile world, social attachments are rarely this comprehensive and integral (and probably never were), community defined thus could only be an increasing rarity in contemporary circumstances. Yet the emotions attributed to collective attachments have hardly disappeared.

An attempt to account for this apparent paradox has been to stress the imagined or symbolic nature of community. All of the chapters in this volume acknowledge the conceptual, imagined dimension of the construction of communities, large or small. Yet when this idea of community is not also invested with social content and context, that is to say when it is not realized in actual social relations, it is difficult to account for the emotive valence which is attributed to it. If the sense of community is primarily or even only ideational, it is difficult to understand the apparent willingness, 'for so many millions of people, not so much to kill, as willingly to die for such limited imaginings', as Benedict Anderson has contended in applying the concept of community to nationalism (1983/1991: 7). We are left with, respectively, an idea and an intense loyalty, but the connection between them is left hanging, an attribute of history or 'cultural roots' that appears to imprison participants rather than be driven by them. In that hiatus between idea and action:

> Individuals come to be analytically treated as incidental to their social relationships and cultural institutions. But to ignore individual

consciousness in this way, to seek simply to read it off from socio-cultural forces and forms, is to exaggerate individuals' vulnerability to these latter and underestimate their resilience.

(Rapport, Chapter 8)

It is this gap, however, which this volume seeks to elucidate. All of the ethnographic cases described in the following chapters insist that the emotive impact of community, the capacity for empathy and affinity, arise not just out of an imagined community, but in the dynamic inter-action between that concept and the actual and limited social relations and practices through which it is realized. People care because they asso-ciate the idea of community with people they know, with whom they have shared experiences, activities, places and/or histories. In turn, they use these interpersonal relations to interpret their relationship to more extended social categories. But at the same time, as noted above, these are not accounts of community as comprehensive, self-sufficient entities. The essential contingency of community, its participants' sense that it is fragile, changing, partial and only one of a number of competing attach-ments or alternative possibilities for affiliation means that it can never be all-enveloping or entirely blinkering. Community is never the world entire, it is only ever one of a number of recognized possibilities.

In this volume we therefore combine affect with Nigel Rapport's (and Anthony Cohen's, 1994) focus on self-consciousness. With self-consciousness comes accountability and rights. Nigel Rapport argues in this volume that individuals must have the 'right to resist and opt out of the norms and expectations of particular social and cultural groupings and chart their own course'. By the same token, knowing that there are always other possibilities, individuals must be accountable for the ways in which they construct community. Thus, when individuals kill or die for the sake of social solidarity, their actions can never be excused or explained away as the exercise of cultural predisposition, ancient enmity or imagined communality. We need to be wary of treating the moraliz-ing rhetoric that is often associated with the assertion of community loyalties as the basis of our own analysis. Community arises out of an interaction between the imagination of solidarity and its realization through social relations and is invested both with powerful affect as well as contingency, and therefore with both consciousness and choice.

In this volume we have therefore attempted to rebalance some of the polarizing tendencies which have featured in scholarly discourses of com-munity. Here is a vision of community that combines the tenuous and fragmented scenarios that were featured in the Rhodes Livingstone accounts of emerging Copperbelt urban communities with the more visceral sense of community stressed by Anthony Cohen in his earlier work. It is an attempt to re-emphasize the social dimensions of community while acknowledging the conceptual elements that have featured so strongly in recent scholarly discourses on this subject. It is also an attempt to balance consideration of the complex processes of constructing collective social attachments with the juxtapositions of contrasting solidarities – that is, the core with the boundary of community, to use John Gray's terms. This is a more modest vision of community but one that does not bemoan the lack of authenticity in its contemporary invocations or reduce them to free floating ideas. Community matters, but it is never everything.

Note

1 I would like to thank Noel Dyck for his helpful comments on, and careful reading of, this chapter.

References

Amit, Vered (editor) (2000) *Constructing the Field: Ethnographic Fieldwork in the Contemporary World.* New York and London: Routledge.

Anderson, Benedict (1983/1991) *Imagined Communities: Reflections on the Origin and Spread of Nationalism.* London and New York: Verso.

Appadurai, Arjun (1996) *Modernity at Large. Cultural Dimensions of Globalisation.* Minneapolis: University of Minnesota Press.

Barth, Fredrik (1969) 'Introduction' to F. Barth (editor) *Ethnic Groups and Boundaries,* pp. 9–38. London: George Allen and Unwin.

Baumann, Gerd (1996) *Constesting Culture: Discourses of Identity in Multi-Ethnic London.* Cambridge: Cambridge University Press.

Chorney, Harold (1990) *City of Dreams: Social Theory and the Urban Experience.* Scarborough, Ontario: Nelson Canada.

Clifford, James and George E. Marcus (editors) (1986) *Writing Culture: The Poetics and Politics of Ethnography.* Berkeley: University of California Press.

Cohen, Anthony P. (1982) 'Belonging: the experience of culture', in Anthony P. Cohen (editor) *Belonging: Identity and Social Organisation in British Rural Cultures,* pp. 1–17. Manchester: Manchester University Press.

—— (1985) *The Symbolic Construction of Community.* London and New York: Tavistock Publications.

—— (1994) *Self Consciousness: An Alternative Anthropology of Identity.* London: Routledge.

Epstein, A. L. (1958) *Politics in an Urban African Community.* Manchester: Manchester University Press.

—— (1964) 'Urban Communities in Africa', in Max Gluckman (editor) *Closed Systems and Open Minds: The Limits of Naïvety in Social Anthropology*, pp. 83–102. Chicago: Aldine.

—— (1978) *Ethos and Identity: Three Studies in Ethnicity*. London: Tavistock.

Evans-Pritchard, E. E. (1940) *The Nuer: A Description of the Modes of Livelihood and Political Institutions of a Nilotic People*. Oxford: Clarendon Press.

Gans, Herbert J. (1962) *The Urban Villagers*. New York: Free Press.

Geertz, Clifford (1973) *The Interpretation of Cultures*. New York: Basic Books.

Gupta, Akhil and James Ferguson (1992) 'Beyond "Culture": Space, Identity and the Politics of Difference', *Cultural Anthropology*, 7(1): 6–23.

Hannerz, Ulf (1980) *Exploring the City: Inquiries Toward an Urban Anthropology*. New York: Columbia University Press.

Herzfeld, Michael (1997) *Cultural Intimacy: Social Poetics in the Nation-State*. New York and London: Routledge.

Hillery, G. A. (1955) 'Definitions of Community: Areas of Agreement', *Rural Sociology*, 20: 86–118.

Lash, Scott and John Urry (1994) *Economies of Signs and Spaces*. London and Thousand Oaks, Calif: Sage.

Lewis, Oscar (1965) 'Further Observations on the Folk-Urban Continuum and Urbanization with Special Reference to Mexico City', in Philip M. Hauser and Leo F. Schnore (editors) *The Study of Urbanization*, pp. 491–517. New York: John Wiley & Sons.

Lustiger-Thaler, Henri (1994) 'Community and Social Practices: The Contingency of Everyday Life', in Vered Amit-Talai and Henri Lustiger-Thaler (editors) *Urban Lives: Fragmentation and Resistance*, pp. 20–44. Toronto: McClelland & Stewart Inc.

Marcus, George E. and Michael M. J. Fischer (1986) *Anthropology as Cultural Critique: An Experimental Moment in the Human Sciences*. Chicago: University of Chicago Press.

Mead, Margaret (1930/1942) *Growing Up in New Guinea*. Harmondsworth, Middlesex: Penguin Books.

Mitchell, J. Clyde (1956) *The Kalela Dance*. Rhodes-Livingstone Papers, no. 27. Manchester: Manchester University Press.

Olwig, Karen Fog and Kirsten Hastrup (editors) (1997) *Siting Culture: The Shifting Anthropological Object*. London and New York: Routledge.

Park, Robert E. (1925) 'The City: Suggestions for the Investigation of Human Behavior', in R. E. Park, W. Burgess and R. D. McKenzie, *The City*, pp. 1–46. Chicago: University of Chicago Press.

Wirth, Louis (1938) 'Urbanism as a Way of Life', *American Journal of Sociology*, 44: 1–24.

Young, Michael and Peter Willmott (1957/1962) *Family and Kinship in East London*. Harmondsworth, Middlesex: Penguin Books.

Chapter 2

The mining community and the ageing body

Towards a phenomenology of community?

Andrew Dawson

Introduction

Why is community so often a potent topic of interest amongst elderly people? Following Cohen's lead (1987), I, like many others, have explained the interest in terms of community providing a cultural resource for mediating change, including the changes wrought by bodily ageing (1990). However, this begs a rather obvious question. Bodily ageing is a central, and perhaps the central, experience in the lives of most elderly people. Why, then, have few if any accounts considered seriously the extent to which the experience of bodily ageing itself might be constitutive of elderly people's senses of community. Focusing on the participants in a range of clubs for the elderly in Ashington, a former coal-mining town in North East England, this chapter considers the relationship between community and bodily ageing, and in particular the experience of mental and physical decline. I offer an account that represents community amongst the elderly simultaneously as a cultural resource and an idea and practice that emerges, in part, from the materiality of bodily experience. More generally, utilizing the work of Thomas Csordas (1994) and, in particular, his use of Merleau-Ponty's idea of 'being-in-the-world' (1962), I question the social constructionist simplicities of most anthropological approaches to community and consider the possibility of a phenomenology of community. After a brief description of contexts the paper moves on to explore, in turn, local ideas and practices surrounding bodily ageing, community and the relationship between bodily ageing and community, and then concludes with an analysis and short theoretical discussion.

Ashington and its clubs for the elderly

In the early part of this century Ashington was commonly referred to as 'the biggest coal-mining village in the world'. However, by 1987 only one pit was in full operation, and 1999 saw the final and cruellest blow. Great hope was placed on the promise of massive investment to develop mining of the vast stocks of undersea coal at the last remaining pit. However, when it became clearer that the behind-the-scenes investor was probably Arkan, the notorious Serbian war criminal, and that the money may have been soaked in blood, unions and management opted for redeployment over investment. The first significant event of the new millennium in Ashington was the announcement of the probable closure of its last pit and the end of an industry that had brought the town's very inception some two hundred years previously.

Ashington is almost a mining town without a mine and, in the absence of any other significant source of employment, its population profile is rapidly ageing. Importantly, as people both leave younger and live longer there is a burgeoning population of elderly people with a lot of time on their hands. Unsurprisingly, there is also a commensurate growth in the number of leisure clubs for the elderly. Some, such as the many working-men's clubs, just happen to be used largely by the elderly. Others, the largest majority and the main focus of this study, are designed specifically for the elderly.

One or two relevant points should be mentioned about the organization and activities of these places. First, while sponsored in part by social services and/or charitable bodies, they are run by elderly participants, and, in line with the principals of the co-operative movement which is firmly established in the area, they tend to be organized democratically and collectively. Secondly, sponsorship by social services and local charities is contingent upon their operation of membership criteria. Central amongst these is the stipulation that they are for the 'active elderly' (NCHC, 1987: 3). This particular membership criterion is designed to ensure that participants are not forced into unwanted care relationships with fellow participants, and if it is not being adhered to, the sponsoring bodies retain rights to intervene in club matters and can withdraw funding. The term 'active elderly' is ill defined. Even the one key strand that is understood by all, that members should not display significant signs of incontinence is rather woolly; one wo/man's incontinence is another's mishap. In practice, definition shifts according to geography. Most obviously, the clubs that are located proximate to, and draw the bulk of their membership from, residential homes are less likely to operate a rigid definition of the term. It also shifts according to those who wish to use it, to include friends, to exclude unwanted members, and to justify or resist the intervention of sponsoring bodies in club affairs. Finally, and most importantly, there is a considerable creative and performative dimension within club life. Many participants engage in the making, writing and/or performance of handicrafts, sketches, dance, songs and, above all, poetry. Indeed, the description of a club as 'a bingo and chat place' is widely used shorthand for a bad club. This represents part of the continuity of a local tradition of artistic creativity that was established in the miner's welfare associations and championed by a modernist urban intellectual elite in the early part of the twentieth century (see Fever, 1988).

The central topic for celebration within the sketches, dance, songs and poetry is unquestionably community. This is hardly surprising. If community is often a potent topic of interest amongst elderly people, then the participants within Ashington's clubs for the elderly have more reason to be interested in it than most. Participating in associations for the elderly involves the construction of *communitas* (Okely, 1990). Here, as in much ritual, songs mark entry to and exit from a world of comradeship borne of shared condition:

> Here we are again,
> Happy as can be,
> All good friends,
> And jolly good company.

And

> Just like Darby and Joan,
> In a world of our own,
> We'll build a nest,
> Way in the west,
> Be it so humble,
> We'll never grumble.
>
> Though the grey locks are showing,
> And the dark clouds are drawing,
> Fear won't betide us,
> Our love will guide us,
> Just like Darby and Joan.

More importantly, while fewer and fewer of its elderly population can claim direct erstwhile involvement in the industry, Ashington is a former coal-mining town, and, as the literature rightly informs us, coal-mining communities are commonly represented as exemplars of the English 'working-class community' *par exellence* (Bulmer, 1975). Having said that community is the central topic for celebration within the clubs, it is followed closely by questions of ageing and, in particular, bodily ageing.

Bodily ageing: Learning to 'age well'

From the moment of joining, participating in the clubs involves learning to 'age well'. In common usage this refers to avoidance of the rigours of bodily ageing. In conscious contradistinction to this, it is used in the clubs to describe those who display successfully a range of outlooks on bodily ageing. Principal amongst these is the perception of mental and physical decline as manageable and, to an extent, controllable.

Management of mental and physical decline is encouraged at both informal and formal levels of club life. Much of the conversation is barely disguised allegory. Its content is often simultaneously political, moral and social. For example, failure to manage or control mental and physical decline results in serious illness and, in turn, wastage of tax-payers' money, deprivation of medical resources to the more deserving and a hastening of the burden of care. Participants are classified as either 'bad or good agers' and vilified or praised accordingly. Constant activity is regarded as a key quality of the good ager and, in practice, as club policy intends, through their adoption of active roles within the clubs most participants are able to act as mutual exemplars of good ageing. However, prime exemplars are accorded an almost totemic and sometimes mythological status. Principal amongst these are the concert party members. These organizations, whose names draw always on metaphors of life, tour the local 'old-aged pensioner' (OAP) club circuit. Their members face often considerable physical demands. Indeed, individual stardom on the scene has more to do with these demands than it has with performative skill. 'Stan-the-Man' Cowton, the opera singer from 'The Springtime Quartet', was a case in point. After between two and ten heart attacks, depending on who you speak to, and the constant threat of more, he would 'raise the rafters off while he was popping them heart pills' and 'sing them high notes so you'd think his heart was going to burst'. At best, being considered as a totem of good ageing is a source of cultural capital. At worst, it is oppressive. During my stay Stan only turned up once. Living up to the hyperbole would, he claimed, 'be the death of me'.

Jack 'Wor Jackie' Coombs, the undisputed star turn in the

'Evergreens', is amongst the most revered in the local OAP club circuit. His life, celebrated through autobiographical poetry, is regarded widely as instructive for good ageing. The poems have a thematic consistency. They characterize Jack as a mental and physical oddity, an intellectual lightweight with a hunched back and epilepsy. As a consequence, he is sexually marginal in particular and marginal within the local community in general. However, despite or, indeed, because of this marginality, he is wise and possesses a cunning sense that prevents him from being taken advantage of:

> Aa'm Jack the humpy-backed coal man,
> Folk think Aa'm not mentally strang,
> Aa shovel coals in for a livin',
> So mebbie they're reit, mebbie wrang.

> Aa hevn't had verry much schoolin',
> Me sums used to drive teacher mad,
> But Aa knaa, if Aa'm paid just two pennies,
> Instead o'three, Aa hev been had.

> Aa mind once the widow, aad Keeney,
> Wad pay me wi' breed and plum jam,
> 'But ye canna buy beer wi' that, hinny',
> Aa says, 'Aa'm a fully grown man'.

> She whimpered, 'Aa'm just a poor widow',
> But Aa knew that hor stockin' was full,
> 'Cos she lay iv'ry neit wi' strange bodies,
> Not me though, Aa'm not sic a fyul.

> She still wadn't pay me ma money,
> So, before ye, not me, could coont ten,
> Aa climbed back into the bowly,
> And hoyed aall the coals oot agyen.

> That larnt the aad besom a lesson,
> For the coals were scattered aal ower,
> And the man that refilled them, charged her,
> Not me three clarty pennies, but fower.

> Aa shud hev mentioned this sooner,
> Aa've been tekin' fits aall me life,
> And Aa think that that is the reason
> Ne lass fancied bein' me wife.

Aa'm aad noo and iver se weary,
The leit in me eyes gettin' dull,
And sumtimes Aa worry, and wunder,
What's gan t' becum of me shul.

Aa'd like it set up as a heedstone,
(When me ingine stops deed in its track),
Wi' these simple words engraved on't,
'To the mem'ry of humpty-backed Jack'.

The significance of Jack's autobiographical poetry is that it resonates with some of the experiences of ageing and reinforces a metaphorical inversion that is central within club life. Mental and physical decline and their resultant marginality, which may be characterized as weaknesses, are in fact characterized as sources of strength. To an extent this process corresponds with Turner's description of the marginal in his development of the notion of *communitas* (1969: 109–10). Similarly, and more to the point, Postal highlights the commonality of representations of the fragile as possessing 'inner strength' (1978: 129).

The inversion informs a number of aspects of club life. It informs informal political strategy. For example, sponsoring bodies, who may be concerned about particular clubs or who may wish to use them as training grounds, often send in staff and volunteers to 'assist' in their running. In response, the elderly organizer-participants use their perceived mental and physical weaknesses in order to undermine this threat to their autonomy. Poor memory is invoked to explain why prearranged meetings did not take place, and poor eyesight is invoked to explain how irrevocable misunderstandings about the clubs' semi-autonomous status emerged (see Dawson in Hockey and James, 1993: 151–2). Clearly, one of the most potent 'weapons of the weak' (Scott, 1985) is weakness itself.

Crucially, the inversion informs informal strategies whose aim is to demonstrate how the ability to manage mental and physical decline is an inherent potentiality. That potentiality stems from an awareness and experiencing of a distance between self and mind and body that emerges through bodily ageing. My observations in this respect are resonant with Leder's phenomenological writing on the body (1990). He contrasts everyday life experience of the body in conditions of well-being and illness. In the former the body *disappears* from awareness. In the latter we become acutely conscious of the body as a kind of *dys-appearance*. We experience, in other words, a bodily alienation or absence.

The awareness and experiencing of distance between self and mind and body is articulated in a number of ways. However, most commonly, the second or third person is deployed for spelling mind and body. In this way, the sense of distance is expressed clearly by two club participants, Jean and Barbara:

Jean: It's a funny thing, when the old age sets in. I don't really know how to put it. Well, I used to just get up in the morning. Now I have this feeling of getting myself up.

Barbara: Aa think to meself, 'wey Barbara, another day with this bloody body of yours'. It's gettin' that Aa have to drag meself everywhere noowadays.

In this way also the self is sometimes presented in a hierarchical relationship with mind and body, a transcendent self over mind and body. At one level this would seem to represent the basis for a means of coping with the rigours of mental and physical decline:

Jean: My legs pain me terribly. I know it's just old age. It's a funny thing. I don't really know how to put it. You just sort of rise above it. I think back to when I had kids. Our first was a terrible screamer. He drove me crazy. Nothing I did could make him stop. It really got me down. Then I realised that ignoring him was the only way to deal with it. I used to shut him out in the back yard. I'm nearly sure all that crying did his lungs the power of good. Well, I do the same with my legs if you get my meaning. When they start playing up, I look at them, say 'Oh, it's you again', and then I just shut them out.

At another level it would seem to represent a basis for managing and, to an extent, controlling mental and physical decline:

Hilda: Aa'm forever forgetting things. Aa'd forget me own hoose if it wasn't for the son ferrying us here and there. Aa hev to tell meself what a fool Aa am. 'Are ee reit in the heed hinny', and 'pull yarself together woman'. That's me way to get by. If Aa tell meself, 'Hilda hinny, yar weakinin and there's nout ye can dee', Aa'll not be long for this earth. Tell meself, 'Hilda hinny, keep on gannin', and Aa'll keep on gannin.

Finally, the self is sometimes presented as transgressive of the bodily boundary, both temporally and spatially. For example, Jimmy Thompson, who was crippled by arthritis, would refer to his body dismissively as 'this thing', 'that thing' or, when in pain, 'him again'. He spoke very differently about himself, 'me', something that had little to do with his body. The self/body transgression had a temporal dimension. He would use dynamic adjectives and mix past and present in the construction of positive narratives of self which stood in sharp relief to his current condition of immobility. It also had a spatial dimension. After spending more than a year with Jimmy on almost a daily basis, I was surprised when he asked me for a walk so that I 'could get to know' him. The walk, with me pushing the wheelchair, turned out to be a tour of his life's achievements. We went from his home to the allotment that was now lovingly tended by his son and then on to the library that housed the collection of figurine pipes he had fired in the brickwork's ovens. His own figurine was placed between Bevan and Stalin, and way to the left of Churchill, 'just so that everyone can see how Aa hang' (his political persuasion). In the event, the walk as a means of me getting to know him made complete sense, for it was in family and material objects, rather than in the body, that Jimmy regarded his self as properly located.

Some participants offer elaborated ideas on how to age well. Most, in their construction, draw explicitly on the experience of a transcendence of self over mind and body. And most, in their dissemination, are related to the comments of others where the second person is used for spelling mind and body. For example, Charlie 'the Preacher' Burnsey explains to anyone who wants to listen that each one of us has an 'aura' which selects our thoughts and sensations. By telling ourselves that 'these feelings are not mine', thoughts of depression and sensations of pain will disappear, but only if we know how to get in touch with our aura. This ability comes only through experience, learning and practice, and through the experience of illness in particular. Thus, he explains, of the many ailments he has had to live with, it is only those that originate in his youth, at a time when he was not practised in contacting his aura, which persistently bother him and will eventually kill him.

The efficacy of the potent mixture of organizational activity, conversation, preaching and entertainment is made clear in participants' comments. One woman explained to me that she could 'be in a bad fettle aall week until club night comes around'. Another explained that her one non-club night was her 'sickly night'. It creates a euphoric atmosphere of well-being which constitutes, at least temporarily, I would argue, a symbolic mastery over bodily ageing, over mental and physical decline.

Community: Difference and sameness

The anthropologist James Brow comments: 'Differences among those who are incorporated within a community are often muted or obscured, while differences between insiders and outsiders are loudly affirmed' (1990: 3).

Ideas of difference and sameness are integral elements within the dominant images of community celebrated within the clubs.

Difference

The dominant image of community that emerges within the clubs is highly segmented. Urban, industrial and working-class Ashington's most significant others are the rural, agricultural and increasingly middle-class areas that surround it, and, beyond that, 'Doon Sooth'. Much is made of the uniqueness of locality and, in particular, of its people's language and dialect, their drinking habits, and their association with the dirt of the coal-mining industry.

From these, a series of largely negative putative images are generated. However, the pertinence of such images is not contested. Instead, their significance is transformed and represented as misunderstood by the putative other, usually the 'Southerner'. Thus, local people's linguistic incomprehensibility is commonly represented as a result of cosmopolitanism rather than isolation and an indication of cleverness rather than ignorance. Local language and dialect is commonly described as the 'Polyglotal Buzz' or, more commonly, the 'Pitmatic'. The former refers to the multifarious inputs to local language and accent brought by the disparate array of migrants who first settled in the area. The latter refers to a dynamic process whereby mining terminology is inventively transformed for metaphorical usage in the description of everyday reality. For example, to emotionally wound someone is to 'hedgehog' them. One of the most common deaths in the pit comes when ones 'guts are ripped out' by a 'hedgehog', the ball of spikes that accumulates on frayed metal cable, when winding gear is travelling at speed. Similarly, the mining man's love of beer is represented less as an indication of his hedonism and more as a sign of his sociability. Its Pitmatic name is 'discourse oil'. Alternatively, it is represented as an essential compensation for a hard working life:

Then buzzer blaas and man to man they queue in front the cage,
For ten lang hoors belaa they'll gan te mek a livin' wage.

> So who amang ya wad begrudge if Saturday neit he boozes,
> Aye, who amang ya wad begrudge that comfort if he chooses.

Most importantly, the significance of the dirt of the mining industry is inverted. A linguistic and symbolic distinction is made between types of dirt. Coal dust, termed 'duff', is pure. Other types of dirt, termed 'muck' or 'clarts' are impure. One popular local poem typifies the distinction:

> There's sum folk wad say that Aa'm dorty,
> For me tyebl'e the back o' me shull,
> But duff's not dorty like muck is,
> Aall pitmen for heartborn suck coal.

The distinction informs several areas of social life, from systems of animal classification to practices designed to ensure pit safety, to ideas about gender and sexuality, and to alternative status hierarchies (Dawson, 1990). The 'stone man', who clears the coal seam of non-coal substances, is held in considerably higher esteem than the ordinary miner precisely because he is regarded, even in this area where coal dust induced pneumoconiosis is rife, as working with substances more dangerous than coal. Thus, while the dirt of the mining industry may be a symbol of marginality, it is also a cherished mark of identity.

Sameness

Sameness between members of the community is represented as rooted at a number of levels. At one level it is a consequence of political and economic circumstance. Explanations of the exploitation that the people of Ashington have suffered resonate with the segmentarist worldview. Northern endeavour has fuelled Southern wealth and, largely because of its location in Westminster, government has persistently favoured the South and neglected the North. Indeed, this neglect is one of the reasons why community, as opposed to the atomism of the South, is regarded as a prevalent feature of Northern life. The much cherished institutions that are regarded as constituting a historic part of community life, from the non-profit making working-men's clubs to the networks of care and assistance, to the unpaid roles people took as community midwives, mourners, vigilantes and so on, are represented commonly as a necessary response to this neglect (Dawson, 1998: 210–11). In essence, in celebrating community, participants within the clubs offer an image of the mutuality of the oppressed.

At another level, the sameness is political and cultural. Participants are aware of sharing an identity whose public representation swings between the revered and reviled. The negative and, indeed, controlling putative images I have described found ultimate confirmation in the early 1980s. In 1983 and in what amounted to a quasi-military operation designed to crush the miner's strike, its members were effectively denied the freedom of movement. For local people whose cars were stopped, searched and denied right of way on the main arterial routes to Britain's coal-fields, speaking the Pitmatic became a kind of anti-passport. Historically, the 'mining community' has played a central role in a range of political discourses, from key locus of proletarian insurrection in revolutionary Marxism to exemplar of community-mindedness in Labourist Communitarianism (Kenny, 1995). In 1983 local people became practically aware of the mining community's Thatcherite depiction as 'the enemy within'.

Finally, and importantly, sameness is represented as generational. Much of the conversation and celebration within the clubs contrasts the shared community-mindedness of the local elderly with the selfish individualism of younger generations. In some expressions this is an end of era story with a persuasive social logic. The end of mining, the community's central referent, was bound to threaten the end of community. Having said this, sameness and, in turn, community is also represented as a consequence of bodily ageing. Most straightforwardly, talk amongst the elderly about bodily ageing leads to their self-identification as a common-interest group. Similarly, their mutual participation in the activities surrounding management of bodily ageing, visiting clinics, picking-up prescriptions and so on, yields new social contacts. However, the communal quality that these relations take on is often more intimately related to the actual experience of bodily ageing, the experience of mental and physical decline and not just what goes on socially around them. At one level, the experience is often characterized as serving to militate against conditions that disrupt community. Above all, it is often described as involving an escape from the biological urges, and in particular the sexual urges, which lie at the root of much conflict. While sharing my urinal space in a club frequented by older men of the town, one regular explained humorously, 'now this kidda is the brag room, and braggin' is the source of aall trouble'. And, whilst looking down forlornly at the place where his manhood once stood proud, 'wey, as you can see, there's nee need for braggin' noowadays, so there's nee reason for trouble neither'.

At another level, the experience is often characterized as the very basis of community. The point is best illustrated with reference to ethnographic vignette.

Hilda's story

Apart from entertainment the main activity within the clubs consists of sitting in groups, drinking tea and chatting. As a first rate raconteur Hilda Blades was a much sought after presence at almost all the tables. She specialized in sexual *double entendre* and stories about past goings-on in the bedrooms of the colliery rows. Though she never said it, others were in little doubt that she was usually at the centre of many of her stories. Unfortunately, Hilda faced in exaggerated form a problem faced by many of the elderly club participants. Diagnosed as suffering from Alzheimer's, her memory was failing rapidly. She also faced in exaggerated form the response which participants with failing memories tend to face. In the early stages of her illness she persisted in telling her stories. When her memory failed her, others would chip in either by prompting her, by filling in the gaps or, in time, by telling the stories themselves with Hilda doing the prompting and gap filling. Hilda became increasingly aware of her diminishing powers as a raconteur and, while continuing to attend the clubs, she became a more passive and silent presence. Concerned about the change, it was suggested that Hilda might find an avenue for the love of performance that failing memory had taken from her by participating in a concert party. At their Christmas show the Evergreens introduced a new act. Hilda 'the hormone' Blades, dressed in suspenders, fishnet stockings and bloomers, danced suggestively with Andy 'the toy boy' Dawson to Madonna's 'Like a Virgin'. The act and the memory of it became a cue for the reconstruction and retelling of Hilda's salacious stories and the telling of stories about Hilda. The stories carried on long after her death.

Mr M's story

Through its juxtaposition of the sexual young woman and the incontinent old woman the image which Hilda performed emphasized the absurdity of sexuality in old age. Confrontation of the changes wrought by ageing through self-deprecating humour is regarded widely within the clubs as another key quality of a good ager. Entertainment and conversation is infused with a wide array of humour focusing on the issues of sex, death and, above all, bodily decline. The latter focuses substantially on the issue of bodily excreta. It is sometimes characterized by conventional scatology, but more usually by the issue of incontinence. For example, Ida, Kate and the Mary's, the Evergreen's 'Buds of May', danced and cancanned to reveal the incontinence pants worn beneath their tutus. In so doing they gave a humorous twist to the music which accompanied them, Diana Ross' gay anthem, 'I'm coming out . . . I want the world to know got to let it show'.

It was no coincidence that this one-off performance took place on one of their rare visits to the Bothal Darby and Joan. The club was facing fairly serious problems. Membership had been ageing and dwindling for some time, activities had tailed off considerably and the participants had split into two not antagonistic camps. One group, most of whom came from the sheltered home next to which the club was located, sat together in the main by-day school hall talking and playing bingo. The other smaller group of women, who had assumed the running of the club, tended to sit in the kitchen talking, playing cards and drinking gin. Despite this, the situation suited most of the participants. However, they were all aware of the dangers it entailed. Matters came to a head towards the end of my stay. One of the few male participants, Mr M suffered an incontinence problem. He tried, usually ineffectively, to conceal matters when he was 'caught short'. However, a discreet search of the corridors leading to the male toilets became an end of evening routine for the organizers. On one occasion, however, the search party missed their target and it was spotted the next day by the hall caretaker. The matter was reported and an appointment made for an inspection by the sponsor, the Women's Royal Voluntary Service. The fears of participants were twofold, either that the club as a whole would fall foul of the 'active elderly' criterion, or that Mr M would face the embarrassing prospect of exclusion. In either case, the risk of closure was real. Few clubs can survive without financial support or the presence of a significant number of men (see Dawson, 1990). In response, the Evergreens were drafted in from another club for the night of the inspection. Their presence lent the club an air of activity. The performance of the Buds of May made light of the problem of incontinence, served to undermine the association between inactive elderly and incontinence and, importantly, sent a message of (organic) solidarity to the embarrassed Mr M. In the event, reprieves offered to Mr M and the club turned out to be short-lived.

Conclusion: From body to community – dying and the 'search' for a home for the self

In a series of publications (1990, 1993, 1994a, 1994b) Thomas Csordas develops a thoroughgoing critique of the representational bias in conventional social theorizing of the body.[1] He calls for recognition of the body's role as a generative source of self and culture rather than as a *tabula rasa* upon which meaning is inscribed. Turning to phenomenology he adopts Merleau-Ponty's idea of 'being-in-the-world' (1962). Here is an approach that captures the mutualism of bodies, selves and cultures. Here, in Csordas' words is an approach that captures existential immediacy in a double sense:

> not as a synchronic moment of the ethnographic present but as temporally/historically informed sensory presence and engagement; and not in the sense of a precultural universalism but in the sense of [a] preobjective reservoir of meaning.
>
> (1994b: 10)

At the heart of this chapter, it might appear, is an attempt to take Csordas' argument into new territory, an attempt to represent the mutualism of body and self and community. Central to my analysis are, first, the contrasting ideas of difference and sameness that form an integral part of notions of community and, second the experience of distance between self and mind and body wrought by bodily ageing.

At one level, amongst several, the distance between self and mind and body that comes through bodily ageing, through mental and physical decline is expressed as a hierarchical relationship, as involving the transcendence of self over mind and body. Within this context, community acts as a cultural resource with which to conceptualize the body and bodily experience. The transcendence of self over mind and body is commonly represented as a basis for managing and, to an extent, controlling that very bodily ageing. Thus, an apparent weakness of the elderly is represented as a source of strength. Importantly, I would argue, in this context at least, ideas about community, ideas of difference and the transformation of putative images of community, provide a master lietmotiv for the metaphorical inversion of weakness into strength.

At another level, the distance between self and mind and body that comes through bodily ageing is expressed as the self trangressing the boundaries of the individual body. It is within this context that we may begin to understand community as an idea and practice that emerges also from the materiality of bodily experience. In conditions of modernity, it is widely argued, body and self are commonly conceptualized as individual (Baumann, 1992: 101), autonomous (Becker, 1995: 21; Lawton, 1997: 7), bounded (Lawton, 1997: 7) and subject to self-control (Becker, 1995: 21; Elias, 1985). In a compelling Douglasian account, Caroline Oliver argues that bodily ageing is often associated with the emergence of a boundary trangressing uncontrolled selfhood (1999). With respect to physical decline, incontinence, meaning literally to 'uncontain', becomes a key symbol of this condition (ibid.: 180). With respect to mental decline, the same might be said of failing memory, especially when it is exhibited as a symptom of extreme neural disorders such as Alzheimer's. For example, the sufferer is frequently described as having 'lost him/herself'. Thus, according to Oliver, bodily ageing represents a crisis for modernity and becomes a matter for social control (ibid.: 182–3).

Contrastingly, I would argue, for the elderly people of this context at least, the experience through bodily ageing of a self that transgresses the boundaries of the individual body is as much a matter for celebration as it is for control. Physical and mental decline, dual aspects of the crumbling of the individual body bring with them a sense of the crumbling of the boundary between self and other. This may explain responses in this context to physical decline and, in particular the concern with scatological and incontinence humour. Douglas is correct to suggest that such humour often constitutes a subversive expression of *communitas* amongst those who are subjected to control (1975: 95–104). However, I would suggest, in this context at least, it is a *communitas* rooted in the immediacy of bodily experience. It may also explain responses in this context to mental decline and, in particular, memory loss. As memory fades, responsibility for the construction of narratives of self and, indeed, possession of these narratives of self slip inexorably from individual to community. In essence, the experience through bodily ageing of a self that transgresses the boundaries of the individual body is a matter for celebration precisely because it becomes a basis for the sameness, a merging of individual selves, integral to senses of community.

So far, so trendy. In an era when attacking the Cartesian legacy of schizmaticization, between intellection and sensation and between culture and biology, for example, is all the rage, arguments for the mutuality of community, self and body, and for the recognition of the body's generative role in the production of self and community are very appealing. I could offer a range of warnings against such temptation, but conclude with just one of particular relevance.[2] To recap, I have presented community in Ashington's clubs for the elderly as, simultaneously, a cultural resource with which to conceptualize the body and bodily experience and an idea and practice that emerges also from the materiality of that very bodily experience. Central to this is awareness and experiencing of a distance between self and mind and body that comes through bodily ageing. Here is a bodily experience that is simultaneously re-conceptualized, as transcendent self, as a resource (a strength) by ideas about community and that, as transgressive self, forms a bodily basis for community. Importantly, however, the latter is entirely contingent, in this case on a particular awareness that is central and, arguably, unique to elderly people as a cohort, an awareness of the proximity of death (de Beauvoir, 1972: 9). Here, then, the central role of awareness and experience of transgressive self is as a means of overcoming the threat of temporal discontinuity wrought by impending death (Myerhoff, 1978). It is manifested in the location of self beyond body in, for example, family, material artefacts and narratives.[3] Thus, we can now answer the question, 'why is community so often a potent topic of conversation amongst the elderly?' In the face of its eviction from the body that death brings, a new 'home' for the self is searched for and sometimes found in community.[4]

Notes

1 From Foucauldian depictions of the body as a readable text upon which reality is inscribed to Mary Douglas's treatment of the body as a vehicle for the expression of a reified social rationality.
2 For example, one would wish to answer yes to Rita Astuti's provocative question 'are we all natural dualists?' (2000).
3 In this case this includes the narrative of the ethnographic account. This is why, in this study, with one exception only people's names are not changed.
4 For an account of a situation where temporal continuity through community is denied to elderly people see Hazan (1980).

References

Astuti, R. (2000) 'Are we all natural dualists? A cognitive developmental approach.' The Malinowski Memorial Lecture. Unpublished.

Baumann, Z. (1992) *Mortality, Immortality and Other Life Strategies*. Cambridge: Polity Press.

De Beauvoir, S. (1972) *Old Age*. London: Andre Deutsch Ltd and George Weidenfeld.

Becker, A. E. (1995) *Body, Self and Society*. Philadelphia: University of Pennsylvania Press.

Brow, J. (1990) 'Notes on community and hegemony and the uses of the past', *Anthropological Quarterly*, 63(1): 12–35.

Bulmer, M. (1975), 'Sociological models of the mining community', *Sociological Review*, 23: 61–92.

Cohen, A. P. (1987) *Whalsay: Symbol, Segment and Boundary in a Shetland Island Community*. Manchester: Manchester University Press.

Csordas, T. J. (ed.) (1990) 'Embodiment as a paradigm for anthropology', *Ethnos*, 18: 5–47.

—— (1993) 'Somatic modes of attention.' *Cultural Anthropology* 8: 135–56.

—— (1994a) *The Sacred Self: A Cultural Phenomenology of Charismatic Healing.* Berkeley: University of California Press.

—— (ed.) (1994b) *Embodiment and Experience: The Existential Ground of Culture and Self.* Cambridge: Cambridge University Press.

Dawson, A. (1990) *Ageing and Change in Pit Villages of North East England.* Unpublished Ph.D. thesis, University of Essex.

—— (1998), 'The dislocation of identity: Contestations of 'home community', in Northern England', in Rapport, N. J. and Dawson, A. (eds) *Migrants of Identity: Perceptions of Home in a World of Movement*, pp. 207–21. New York and Oxford: Berg.

Douglas, M. (1975) *Implicit Meanings.* London: Routledge and Kegan Paul.

Elias, N. (1985) *The Loneliness of Dying.* Oxford: Basil Blackwell.

Fever, W. (1988) *The Pitmen Painters: The Ashington Group, 1934–84.* London: Chatto and Windus.

Hallam, E., Hockey, J. and Howarth, G. (1999) *Beyond the Body.* London: Routledge.

Hazan, H. (1980), *The Limbo People: A Study of the Time Universe Among the Aged.* London: Routledge and Kegan Paul.

Hockey, J. and James, A. (1993) *Growing Up and Growing Old: Ageing and Dependency in the Life Course.* London: Sage.

Kenny, M. (1995) *First New Left: British Intellectuals After Stalin.* London: Lawrence and Wishart.

Lawton, J. (1997) 'Hospice care: The sequestration of the unbounded body and dirty dying.' Unpublished.

Leder, D. (1990) *The Absent Body.* Chicago: University of Chicago.

Merleau-Ponty, M. (1962) *Phenomenology of Perception.* James Edie, trans. Evanston, IL: Northwestern University Press.

Myerhoff, B. G. (1978) 'A symbol perfected in death: Continuity and ritual in the life and death of an elderly Jew', in Myerhoff, B. G. and Simic, A. (eds) *Life's Career Aging: Cultural Variations on Growing Old.* London: Sage.

Northumberland Community Health Council (1987) *Guide Around Services for the Local Elderly.* Newcastle-Upon-Tyne: NCHC.

Okely, J. (1990) 'Clubs for the troisieme age: *Communitas* or conflict', in Spencer, P. (ed) *Anthropology and the Riddle of the Sphinx: Paradoxes of Change in the Life Course*, pp. 194–210, London and New York: Routledge.

Oliver, C. (1999) 'Ordering the disorderly', *Education and Ageing*, 14(2): 171–202.

Postal, S. (1978) 'Body image and identity: A comparison of Kwakiutl and Hopi', in Polhemus, T. (ed.) *Social Aspects of the Human Body.* Middlesex: Penguin.

Scott, J. C. (1985) *Weapons of the Weak: Everyday Forms of Peasant Resistance.* New Haven and London: Yale University Press.

Turner, V. W. (1969) *The Ritual Process: Structure and Anti-Structure.* London: Lowe and Brydon.

Chapter 3

Community as place-making

Ram auctions in the Scottish borderland

John Gray

There is a lot of rethinking going on among anthropologists about the relation between people and place that has served as the assumed analytic foundation for some of our most cherished concepts – culture, identity and community – concepts that refer to a 'social sense of spatial distinctiveness' (Nadel-Klein 1991: 501) as well as a spatial sense of social distinctiveness. This rethinking has been brought about by anthropologists perceiving a 'predicament of emplacement' confronting both parties involved in the ethnographic relation.

There is an existential predicament of emplacement experienced by the people whose lives are the focus of ethnography. Anthropologists are continually presented with and presenting to other anthropologists evidence that people are increasingly subject to transnational processes that disrupt their relation to an apparently fixed and identifiable place which is constitutive of self, identity, and/or community and fundamental to being a person-in-the-world (Seamon 1984: 45, Casey 1996). Appadurai's notion of deterritorialization is perhaps the best known and graphic description of the way in which specific territorial boundaries that have been seen as the spatial foundation of culture and forms of group identity are transcended by transnational corporations, large-scale labour migration, global movements of capital and mass communication such that 'groups are no longer tightly territorialised, spatially bounded, historically unselfconscious or culturally homogeneous' (1991: 191). Gupta and Ferguson recognize a similar existential predicament in describing how 'the rapidly expanding and quickening mobility of people combines with the refusal of cultural products and practices to "stay put" . . . give a profound sense of loss of territorial roots, of an erosion of the cultural distinctiveness of place' (1997: 37). Auge's description of the non-places of supermodernity (1995), Basso's portrayal of the dislocating effects of global processes on indigenous peoples (1996), Jackson's journey, through an ethnography of the life-world of Australian Aborigines, to find out 'what it means, in the late twentieth century, to be at home in the world' (1995) and Rapport and Dawson's account of movement and its effects on the people's sense of home (1998) attest to the seeming pervasiveness of the predicament of emplacement that people everywhere are experiencing in their everyday lives. Likewise, there is a reciprocal reflexive predicament of emplacement experienced by anthropologists themselves with regard to their spatialized concepts of culture, identity and community. They are recognizing that the same global processes that dislocate people also dislocate the 'assumed iso-morphism of space, place and culture' (Gupta and Ferguson 1997: 34) and disturb the 'place-focused notion of culture' (Hastrup and Olwig 1997: 5). Hence the need and burgeoning practice of rethinking these concepts.

Hastrup and Olwig (1997: 11) and Gupta and Ferguson (1997: 39) recognize an irony in the reactions to the predicament. Just as anthro-pologists are responding to their reflexive predicament of emplacement by questioning the validity of their place-focused concepts, 'deterritori-alized' peoples are responding to their existential predicament of emplacement by re-emphasizing the inextricability of place in their social lives (see Casey 1996) as they engage in an often self-conscious process of producing a sense of place in a world of movement. Nadel-Klein's analysis of the persistence of localism – 'the continuing reference to place in assertions of a political or cultural will to distinctiveness' (1991: 501) – in Scotland provides a concrete illustration of how the marginal-izing and dislocating effects of a global political economy on local communities paradoxically produces 'representations of group identity as defined primarily by a sense of commitment to a particular place and to a set of cultural practices' . . . (1991: 502). In this respect, place-making remains a fundamental process for humans. Creating a place for one's self and for one's group is central to personal and social existence. Losing one's place because of these global processes may be one of those post-modern ironies that engenders a heightened awareness not only of the place lost, but also of the centrality of being-in-place to self, identity and community.[1]

Community and place-making

As is obvious from these introductory remarks, I will be situating my rethinking of community within this more general predicament of emplacement. In making this assertion, I am proposing that community is both process and product of place-making in which the sense of being in a group – whatever the basis of that sense, for example, shared culture, location, occupation, interest, ethnicity, national identity – and its place emerge simultaneously and are mutually constitutive. I am not suggesting that place-making exhausts the nature of community; rather I am arguing that place-making and the resultant sense of place are an essential part of how people experience community.

As ethnographers, we usually encounter community as a way a group of people refer to their special and shared relation to a geographical space and the place-making practices that create it. The particular characteristics of such a sense and practice of community can vary depending upon (a) the specific historical, social and political circumstances of its production and (b) the social and territorial scope of the referent. Here I am alluding to the variety of social group/place configurations – 'imagined' national (Anderson 1983), ethnic (Blu 1996) and, in the case described here, local – that have been referred to by members and analysts as 'community'. Thus I do not attempt re-conceptualizing a singular concept of community associated with and defined by fixed configuration (or conflation) of social–spatial characteristics that differentiates it from other concepts relating people to place, such as culture and identity. Instead, my aim in this chapter is to describe the particular way in which hill sheep farming people in the Scottish Borders are reformulating their sense of community in response to specific social-historical circumstances that they see as bringing about the decline of their local communities.

There are two remarkable features of their community place-making. The first is that it focuses on what people in Teviothead see as the core of their communityness – a common interest in sheep. As one farmer put it: 'In our agricultural community, there are three classes of people. An individual is in one of these. But all are involved with sheep; it is the common interest which binds everyone in the community.' In contrast, Cohen (1982) and Gupta and Ferguson (1997) emphasize a community's symbolic or physical boundaries. To be fair to Cohen and to Gupta and Ferguson, they do recognize that community includes 'simultaneously both similarity and difference' (Cohen 1982: 12) but both privilege the boundary as the more important of the two in constituting community. Thus, Cohen writes:

> The word [community] expresses a *relational* idea: the opposition of one community to others or to other social entities. Indeed, it will be argued that the use of the word is only occasioned by the desire

or need to express such a distinction. It seems appropriate, therefore, to focus our examination of the nature of community on the element which embodies this sense of discrimination, namely, the *boundary*.

(1982: 12)

Similarly, Gupta and Ferguson argue:

community is never simply the recognition of cultural similarity or social contiguity but a categorical identity that is premised on various forms of exclusion and construction of otherness. This fact is absolutely central . . . for it is precisely through processes of exclusion and othering [what Cohen would call symbolic boundary marking] that both collective and individual subjects are formed. With respect to locality as well, at issue is not simply that one is located in a certain place but that the particular place is set apart from and opposed to other places.

(1997: 13).

One of the themes of my ethnography is that it is not the boundary that is always of paramount concern to the people building a sense of community. Instead, community-making may be founded on what they see as its core meaning, institution, occupation, and/or activity. This difference between an emphasis on the boundary and an emphasis on the core in defining or constituting a community may be indicative of a more general difference between two modes of concept building.[2]

The second remarkable feature is that not only are sheep the core of the sense of community in the Scottish borders, they are also the means of creating its placedness. In the following analysis, I describe a place-making disposition of hill sheep farmers in which sheep act as a mediator, mechanism and metaphor for an embodied or consubstantial relation between a family and a farm. I suggest that, in the context of their declining sense of local community in Teviothead, this same disposition forms the basis for hill sheep farming people to improvise, through their practices in selling rams at the annual auctions in Lockerbie, a geographically expanded sense of their local community in which a way of life – hill sheep farming – and place – the Scottish Borders – are mutually constitutive. The more general point of this dimension of the ethnography is that community involves place-making.[3]

Borders hill farms and sheep

Teviothead consists of between 150 and 200 residents of fifteen hill sheep farms and nearly thirty cottages that straddle an 18 kilometre stretch of the River Teviot from its source in the Border hills to the mill town of Hawick. Three farms are owner occupied, eleven are occupied under tenancy[4] and one is operated by a resident manager employed by an estate. All the owner-occupied and tenanted farms are family farms in that members of a 'family', usually consisting of a married couple and unmarried or recently married children, are the owners of capital (land, buildings, sheep and farm machinery – tenants owning only the latter two forms of capital) and provide a significant proportion of the labour.[5]

The farms lie in the valley of the River Teviot bounded by steep hills reaching 600 metres at the watershed and gradually decreasing in height and density as one moves in a north-westerly direction towards Hawick. They range in size from 160 to over 2,000 hectares carrying 400 to 4,000 breeding ewes.[6] Hill sheep farmers differentiated the physical terrain into two categories of farm land – *outbye* and *inbye* – each suitable for rearing different kinds of sheep. All farms in the valley have some of both types of land. The nine larger farms (over 500 hectares) on the higher ground nearer the watershed have a greater proportion of hill land (more than 75 per cent), and the six smaller farms on generally lower ground have a smaller proportion of hill land (less than 50 per cent).

Outbye, rough grazing or hill land is characterized by steep gradients, altitudes in excess of 300 metres, harsh weather, boggy soil and nutrient-poor vegetation. It is usually unfenced. All farms in Teviothead raise one of two breeds of hill sheep – South Country Cheviot and Blackface – that through selective breeding have become adapted to these conditions and have grazed these hills for hundreds of years. However, while these breeds of hill sheep are adapted to the harsh conditions of outbye land, they tend to produce single births and their relatively small lambs are usually sold to other farms outside the borders for fattening to European Community standards.

Hill sheep have a natural territoriality and hill sheep farming in the Scottish borders is characterized by a distinctive mode of herding (to be described shortly) through which sheep become attached to particular tracts of hill land where they remain throughout their lives. Because they pass on this attachment to their offspring, hill sheep embody the specific locale where they graze. This cultural complex of specific breeds of sheep, distinctive herding techniques and resulting attachment of hill sheep to specific locales has provided the foundation for people in

Teviothead to see themselves as sharing a relatively homogeneous hill sheep farming 'way of life'. As a result, hill sheep are the most important objects mediating the place-making of hill sheep farmers (see Gray 2000).

Inbye or park are areas of lower altitude flat fields that become increasingly prevalent nearer to Hawick. On this type of land, Teviothead farmers raise larger, less hardy cross-bred sheep. Cross-bred sheep have two major commercial advantages over hill sheep: they have a higher rate of multiple births and they are more cost-effectively fattened on inbye pasture to European Community standards. However, because they are kept in fenced fields and are moved from field to field as the grass runs out, they do not become attached to specific locales like hill sheep do. As a result, park sheep are much less important than hill sheep to hill sheep farmers' sense of place and their sense that they share a distinctive way of life.

Place without community

Since I began fieldwork in 1981, the people of Teviothead have experienced a predicament of emplacement. I was told almost from my first day in Teviothead that the community was in decline and that defining its existence and nature had been problematic for a number of years. The most troubling indications of the decline were those affecting their community's central and constitutive institutions: the decreasing numbers of children in the local primary school, the withdrawal of a resident minister from the local kirk, and the state of disrepair of the community hall. Yet, I also found that through their farming practices with hill sheep, people of Teviothead reproduce a strong sense of attachment to their farms and the hills that characterize the landscapes of this region of the Scottish Borders.

Decline of community

In a formal sense, Teviothead refers to a parish and electoral district; it is also what people in the locality use to name their local community. Throughout the 1980s, Teviothead as a community was being explicitly reappraised. There was an ongoing debate among those resident in the valley about whether the formerly separate communities of Teviothead and neighbouring Newmill should be considered as one. Discussions of this issue among people in both locales crystallized around the diminished membership of the Newmill and Teviothead chapters of the

Women's Rural Institute and the Church Guild, the decreased patronage at the three local hotels, and the need for greater participation in the activities sponsored by the separate Newmill and Teviothead Community Hall Committees. All of these were symptoms of the locality's declining population, which they attributed to external forces: the sale of economically marginal farms for forestry plantations and the reduction in number of hired workers that resulted from the European Community Common Agricultural Policy's objectives of introducing technology to farming and a market-oriented drive to reduce production costs.

During this same period, they identified other social and political forces emanating from outside Teviothead that undermined what they saw as the central social institutions – school, kirk and community hall – which in the past had been constitutive of their local farming community. The buildings housing all three institutions are situated centrally in the geographical territory of Teviothead. In this respect, the way in which people in Teviothead describe their community in terms of the socially core institutions located in the territorial centre of the community resembles how Tamils defined their village in terms of important places demarcating its social and spatial centre rather than in terms of its boundaries (Daniel 1984: 74).

School

In the late 1970s, the Teviothead school was organizationally amalgamated with the Hawick schools. As a result, only primary education currently takes place in the local schoolhouse. Older Teviothead children travel eight miles to Hawick for their secondary education. Periodically, there are threats to the local primary school because of the possibility of the Council closing it when the number of pupils decreases due to demographic cycles among the local population. For the people of Teviothead, children attending a local primary school is one of the last and most important institutions for practically defining and reproducing their community: 'The school brings together families – children, parents and grandparents – and neighbours.' One farmer said: 'If the Teviothead school closes down, that will be the end of the community.' Many farmers identified the membership of the community in terms of those people whose children attended the local primary school. A farmer who was relatively new to the locality said: 'My son will be a member of the Teviothead community because he is going to school here.'

Kirk

The Teviothead parish kirk of the Church of Scotland was merged with the parish kirk in Hawick. As a result there is no longer a resident minister and services are conducted in the Teviothead kirk only fortnightly. Like the school, the kirk is important to the practical existence of the community. Reflecting on the loss of a resident minister, one farmer said: 'The minister ran things in the community, like the Whist Drives and Christmas Parties . . . and the minister was the Registrar of births and deaths so he knew everything that was going on in the community.' Another pointed to church rituals as a mechanism of retaining local identity: 'People want to get married and have their funeral in the *local* Kirk.'

Community Hall

By the mid-1980s, the Teviothead Community Hall had fallen into a state of disrepair due to the neglect of Hawick Council. In a practical expression of 'community spirit', it was 'salvaged' by the people of Teviothead who purchased the Hall from the Council for £1.00 thereby assuming all responsibility for its – and the community it represented – refurbishment and maintenance.

European Community and United Kingdom agricultural policies

Local people attributed the relative cultural homogeneity of Teviothead to hill sheep farming – which they understood to be their 'way of life' in the Borders. Hill or outbye sheep (as opposed to inbye or park sheep) – the way of life and place they embody and represent – are central to their sense of community. Farmers and shepherds in Teviothead told me that Border hill sheep farming is distinctive in terms of the breeds of sheep raised, the organization of hill sheep into groups (*heft*) based upon the way they form an enduring attachment to a territory in the hills, the organization of hill shepherding in terms of these territorial groups of sheep (*hirsel*), and the consequent intimate knowledge and identification between people, sheep and place. However, in the 1980s, the introduction of the European Community Sheep Meat Regime, combined with the United Kingdom Agricultural Improvement and Development Grants, led to a differentiation in hill sheep farming in Teviothead that disturbed people's sense of local cultural homogeneity and the distinctiveness of hill sheep farming that was an important part of their sense of community.

The Sheep Meat Regime was essentially a price-support scheme in which the price of lambs was subsidized. Only lambs that fulfil Community-wide certification standards of meat-to-fat ratio and minimum weight are eligible for the subsidy. The United Kingdom Agricultural Improvement and Development Grants provided funding to improve the quality of land through draining, fencing and re-seeding. During the 1980s and early 1990s, most farms in Teviothead used these grants to convert some lower areas of hill land into fenced inbye land.

Prior to the introduction of the Sheep Meat Regime, all Teviothead hill sheep farms maximized profit by maximizing the number of smaller but 'unfinished' hill lambs sold on the store market to buyers who would 'finish' (fatten) them on their farms located in milder climates. These buyers knew the individual hill farms and shepherds in the Borders and tended to buy lambs from particular farms because they knew the lambs from these farms would fatten well on their own farms. Thus, unfattened hill lambs sold on the store market were identified with a specific farm and shepherd and with Borders hill sheep farming.

The way Teviothead farmers adapted to the Sheep Meat Regime and used the development grants led to a diversification within and between their hill sheep farms. Those farms with a high proportion of rugged hill land that could not be converted into improved pasture were unable to switch production from pure-bred hill lambs to cross-bred field lambs. They largely remained 'breeding' farms in the sense that the majority of their production was pure-bred hill lambs. Those farms that had a greater proportion of low-lying hill land and flat fields converted the former to improved pasture where they could raise less-hardy, but more prolific field sheep and where the larger lambs could be fattened to the certification standards of the Sheep Meat Regime. These farms sought to increase the production of cross-bred fat lambs that were eligible for the subsidy. They were labelled 'commercial' farms because there was less emphasis on breeding programmes for pure-bred hill sheep and more emphasis on feeding programmes for cross-bred field sheep.

There are two consequences of EC and UK agricultural policies that contributed to a decline in Teviothead people's sense of local community. First, the diversification into breeding and commercial farms decreased Teviothead people's everyday experience of cultural homogeneity and community that was embedded in distinctive hill sheep and farming practices. Second, EC and UK agricultural policies increased the attractiveness for all farmers in Teviothead of cross-bred lambs sold on the fat market. Unlike the buyers of unfinished store lambs, buyers of fat lambs represent abattoirs who slaughter and distribute the lamb throughout the United Kingdom and Europe. Their only concern is that the lambs fulfil the anonymous and Community-wide standards; they are not interested in knowing the specific farm, shepherd or form of farming that produced them. As a result, cross-bred fat lambs are an anonymous and deterritorialized agricultural commodity that decreases Teviothead farmers' sense of community.

Hill sheep and sense of place

Despite these symptoms of their declining community in terms of population, core institutions and cultural homogeneity and distinctiveness, people in Teviothead maintain a sense of place and attachment to the locality largely through the way hill sheep mediate what might be called a consubstantial relation between themselves and their farms. In a consubstantial relation, two phenomena – in our case a family of humans and a farm as a space of defined land, buildings and animal – seemingly distinct in time, space and/or nature, partake of the same substance and are therefore fundamentally different refractions of one phenomenon. On Teviothead hill sheep farms, there are three aspects of herding through which hill sheep both embody and produce such a consubstantial place-relation between families and farms.

First is the process of '*hefting on*' in which a distinct groups of between fifty and 120 ewes (called a heft) acquires a special bond or attachment to a particular territory on the outbye hill (also called a heft). An essential part of this special attachment is that the ewes remained in the same heft throughout their lives and thereby learn about and adapt to its specific topographical features, vegetation, soils and parasites. Further, replacement stock is selected from the ewe lambs born of the heft so that it consists of a descent line of ewes. As a result, a heft of ewes is understood to genetically incorporate and transmit through selective breeding their acquired adaptations to the specific characteristics of the hill territory and this gives each heft its distinctiveness. In this respect, ewes embody the land upon which they live and are distinguished by it. Second are the herding practices of hill shepherds. Hill shepherds are responsible for a *hirsel* of between 800 and 1,000 ewes from spatially contiguous hefts. Their work routine involves going around the hill two to three times a day during lambing and the following two months, and once a day for the rest of the year. Through such intensive herding, shepherds acquire intimate knowledge of both the topography of the hill land and the individual sheep. As a result, their stockmanship and personhood are seen to be embodied in the hirsel of ewes for which they are responsible. Third is the farm's breeding programme – the selection and rotation of tups (rams) among the hefts of ewes during the mating season in November. This is the responsibility of the farmer; and just like the case of the hill shepherd, the farmer's stockmanship and personhood are embodied in the tups and ultimately in the farm's flock. Thus for both the hill shepherd and the farmer, a descent line of sheep, the personhood of a human being and the characteristics of the land upon which they live became consubstantial – shepherd and hirsel, farmer and farm are united in hill sheep. And this relation between being/s and place is repetitively reproduced every year in the herding and breeding practices that produce hill lambs for sale on the agricultural market.

This ethnographic material on herding and breeding practices suggests that hill sheep are central to hill sheep farmers' sense of place. The relation between humans, hill sheep and the territory is both a lived metaphor (Jackson 1996: 9) and mechanism for a farming family to create a sense of place on a farm. As metaphor, a descent line of sheep – whether heft or flock – bonded to and embodying a particular territory over generations is an iconic image of the sense of place that characterizes the family farm. The metaphor goes further in suggesting how this relation is acquired by a family: a descent line of sheep simultaneously creates a place and its special attachment to it in the act of living and reproducing on it. Moreover, a descent line of sheep is not only an image of the relation between family and farm, but it also mediates the creation of the relation. In everyday herding and breeding activities on hill sheep farms, families became consubstantial with their farms in and through their sheep because both the farm places and the people themselves become consubstantial in the flock.

My point in this section of the chapter has been to describe the current state of Teviothead as a community. Farming people recognize that they have less of a sense or experience *of* Teviothead as their local community now than when children attended primary *and* secondary school locally, when there was a resident minister for the local kirk, and when the Community Hall was in better repair because it was used more frequently for local dances, whist drives, indoor bowls, meetings of the annual Agricultural Show committee and other community events. At the same time, they continually reproduce a strong sense of place *in* Teviothead through their place-making of a consubstantial relation with their farms – and the hills that are their defining topography – mediated by hill sheep. As a result, in relation to the locality called Teviothead, people have a sense of place without community. In the next section of the chapter, I describe how, through this hill sheep-mediated place-making, farming people from Teviothead and other localities throughout the Scottish Borders may be improvising a sense of community among themselves.

Ram auctions

In September, hill sheep farming people from around the Borders gather at the Lockerbie Auction Mart for the annual sale of South Country Cheviot rams. Nearly 500 tups raised by approximately fifty breeders are sold. Each breeder offers between two and twenty tups, with the 'big' breeders having the larger number for sale. While there are other ram auctions in Scotland, the one at Lockerbie relates more closely to hill sheep farming in the Borders region. South Country Cheviot sheep were developed as a breed for Border hill sheep farming to cope with the harsh conditions of outbye land. They are still the breed of hill sheep raised on most Border hill farms. The South Country Cheviot breed is a core object and icon of Borders hill farming in two ways. First and obviously, the name of the breed spatially links these sheep to the Cheviot Hills which are one of the defining features of Border landscapes. Second, through the selective breeding practices of hill sheep farmers over many generations, the breed has gone through a process of biological adaptation to the environmental conditions and landscape of the Border hills. In this respect, South Country Cheviot sheep embody hill sheep farming and its place in the Border hills.[7]

Hill sheep as values

Hill sheep are objects with exchange value and, more importantly, cultural value. As described in the previous sections, hill sheep embody and mediate hill sheep farming people's sense of place. In this mode, they are objects of cultural value because they are endowed with specific meanings that refer to and constitute the specific farmers and shepherds who care for them and to the specific farms on which they are raised.

This self-referential and place-making function is highly developed in tups, particularly those that breeders make into aesthetic objects for sale at the annual Lockerbie auction. In giving tups an aesthetic quality, breeders emphasize their cultural value as symbols of themselves, hill sheep farming and the Scottish Borders, that is, the particular relation they experience between persons, way of life and place that are the ingredients of their sense of community. Like the function that hill sheep play in the family–farm relation described earlier, I suggest in the following analysis that tups are both the mediators and mechanism for the community place-making process that happens in the Lockerbie auction. As we shall see, in the selection and grooming of tups for the Lockerbie auction, tups come to embody the people whose knowledge of sheep and stockmanship skills epitomize hill sheep farming; and, in the pattern of bidding for tups in the auction itself, hill sheep farming people throughout the Borders realize the potential of their tups to create a sense of community among themselves.

Of tups and hill sheep men[8]

One evening after a walk around his hirsel and a meal with Charlie Nixon, a hill shepherd on one of the larger farms, I accompanied him on his final chore of the day – feeding the sale tups. When we arrived at the pens where the tups were kept, Charlie just stood in silence, doing nothing but gazing at them blissfully for nearly ten minutes. I was reminded of Geertz's graphic account of 'cock crazy' Balinese men whose self is expressed in their cocks; and like Balinese men, tup breeders 'spend an enormous amount of time with their favourites, grooming them, feeding them, discussing them, trying them out against one another, or just gazing at them with a mixture of rapt admiration and dreamy self-absorption' (1975: 418–419). Certainly, one of the most respected breeders of South Country Cheviot tups in the Borders made the expressive link between self and tup explicit when he said: 'The Lockerbie Tup Sales is an event when you present your farm and your self to your peers. Your peers view your tups as indicative of you as a farmer and pass judgement on you and your farm in the way they bid on your tups.' As we will see, the more expensive the tups, the more important is their expressive function and the less important their commodity function of producing profit.

Again, like cockfighting in Bali, tup breeding is done by hill sheep men – but not just any hill sheep men. Breeding tups – and being accepted as a serious breeder – is both a privilege and mechanism of eminence such that both sale tups and those who breed them for the Lockerbie auction form the focus of what it means to be a hill sheep farmer in the Borders. Earlier, I described commercial farmers as those who, with respect to raising lambs, were shifting production away from pure-bred hill lambs sold on the store market to cross-bred park lambs sold on the fat market. With respect to tups, the term 'commercial' refers to another dimension of these farmers: they raised and purchased less expensive sale tups (also referred to as 'commercial' tups) or they were the non-tup-breeding farmers who bought them. As one farmer of the latter category ironically put it: 'with tup breeding you are approaching the heights of the gods'.

In Teviothead there were four tup-breeding farms.[9] The farmer of one of them was respected throughout the Borders as one of the best tup breeders not just by the quality of his tups and the prices they fetched, but also by the amount he was willing to spend purchasing tups from other 'big' breeders. Like most of these breeders, he offered at least ten tups for sale each year, recognizing that only two or three of these were the really good ones that other top breeders would buy. The rest were commercial grade tups that the 'commercial men' would buy.

Selecting and grooming tups

The exchange value of tups ultimately lies in the genetic make-up that they will contribute to a farm's flock. The best breeders are renowned for their ability to see in young and undeveloped lambs the genetic potential to grow into a mature tup with the physical characteristics that other tup breeders value and that will produce lambs with the bodily configuration valued by the agricultural market. Of great interest to, and given extra scrutiny by, the most prestigious breeders are the tup lambs from tups bought at previous years' sales because it is these lambs that have the greatest potential to be the high-price tups through which breeders display themselves and their stockmanship to other Borders hill sheep farmers.

These selection practices generate a sense of social centrifugality towards the group of top breeders who have a reputation throughout the Borders for their stockmanship, who epitomize hill sheep farming and who are explicitly referred to as 'the clique'. The social centrifugal logic of tup-breeding practices is a consequence of their genetic involution: those tups bred by top breeders that fetch high prices produce tup lambs that the purchasing breeders tend to select for return to the sales, where they receive high prices as products of top breeders because they were bred from high-price tups of top breeders. The sale catalogue provides some evidence of this closed circulation and escalation of tups, genes and stockmanship skills among the clique of breeders. Every tup sold is listed individually in the sale catalogue and its sire identified. Tups are individually named by breeders and the name of the farm is included in it.

Sire-names, therefore, identify the farm where they are raised so it is always possible to know the recent genealogy of the tup. In analysing the entries in the sale catalogues from seven consecutive Lockerbie auctions, over 90 per cent of the sires of tups sold by breeders whose tups generally received both the highest individual prices (over £1,500) and highest average price (over £450) were raised on the farms of these same breeders.[10] That is, over time the most expensive tups that epitomized Border hill sheep farming and embodied farmers' expertise were bought and sold among a distinct group of breeders.

Since the genetic make-up of tups is determined at conception, breeders also spend a lot of time and effort just prior to the Lockerbie sales grooming their tups to accentuate those characteristics that epitomize hill sheep – hardiness for the harsh outbye environment and a body conformation for a carcass valued on the agricultural market. The tups' horns are shaped with electric sanding machines to reveal as much of the tup's crown as possible – a big crown being a sign of hardiness; the wool is washed, fluffed up with a wire brush and hand clipped to give an overall shape to the appearance of the body: straight back, wide and square back end; the wool is coloured and the faces whitened to enlarge the appearance of the head as another sign of hardiness. The aim of such grooming is to enhance the tups' value as signs of their expert stockmanship in detecting the quality of the tups' genetic make-up and thus as instruments of their reputations as hill sheep farmers. In explaining these practices of appearance, they used a discourse of aesthetics to emphasize the value of tups as cultural objects rather than a discourse of pragmatics that emphasized their value as commodities. As the quotation above (see p. 50) suggests, they recognized that they presented themselves, their stockmanship and their farms for evaluation through their tups.

Under my questioning, breeders admitted that grooming the tups would not fool other breeders, who might buy them, into thinking the animals are better than they actually are. For a couple of hours before the sale, the tups are in holding pens and buyers are able to closely examine them visually and physically. Instead, they said that they wanted to make the tups 'look good for the crowd'.

A circle of visiting

Prior to the Lockerbie auction, there is a period of reciprocal visiting among the big breeders. During this two-week visiting season, breeders bring their sale tups into pens near the farmhouse and most of the evenings are spent gazing at and discussing the tups individually over liberal amounts of whisky. The ostensive purpose of the visiting is to pre-view others breeders' tups. However, those invited to visit are known to be the breeders who in the past had paid high prices for tups from the farms they visit; and the farms they visit are those in the past that had produced tups fetching the highest prices. Over the two weeks, each breeder in the circle is both visited by and visits most of the other breeders in the clique.

There are just over a dozen farms included in the visiting circle and together they form the annually self-perpetuating and socially centrifugal clique. The reciprocal visiting and the resulting group of mutually produced elite breeders includes farms located in the Ettrick, Yarrow, Eskdalemuir, Teviothead, Ewesdale, Annandale valleys. Together these valleys define the geographical locality within the Scottish Borders where hill sheep farming is the major form of agriculture and way of life.

The sales: A circle of differential value

The Lockerbie sales take place every year in late September. Breeders, commercial farmers and shepherds from farms around the Borders attend the auction; it is the major event of hill sheep farmers for hill sheep farmers. Everyone wears their best clothes and brings their show sticks; members of the breeders' families attend and form a large part of the audience. There is a catalogue setting out the temporal order of sale by farm. It identifies the farmer, the farm and its location in the Borders; then the tups being offered for sale are listed in order of the breeder's judgement of their quality – best first – and numbered individually as the consecutive sale lots; and the sire of each tup is named. If one of the sires has a particularly illustrious reputation or had been bought for an especially high price, it is noted at the end of the farm's entry in the catalogue.

Like all auction marts, the spatial layout of the Lockerbie mart is concentrically structured and focused on the sale ring that is bounded by a three-foot wall, around which is a walkway, itself surrounded by several tiers of stands for the audience. The spatial organization of the audience segments them into groups that reflect their knowledge, personal stake in the quality of the tups, and participation in the bidding. In the top tiers of the stands that are furthest from the ring sit the wives, daughters and young children of the breeders. These women 'mark the catalogue', noting down the price and buyer name of every ram sold, not just those from their farm. In the lower tiers of the stand are the commercial farmers, mostly men, who are there to bid for commercial tups that sell for £400 or less. The breeders who are socially closest to the tups are also physically closest to the ring. They take up the best and closest vantage points – they sit on the benches lining the inside of the wall and congregate just outside the exit gates where they can see the tups in the holding pens just prior to their entry into the ring, can see into the ring and can be seen by the auctioneer during the bidding.

For the bidding, each tup is herded into the ring individually by its breeder, highlighting the association of breeder and tup; other of the farm personnel and their friends stay outside to help push each successive tup into the ring in the correct order.[11] At the end of the bidding, the auctioneer announces the final purchase price and identifies the buyer by name.

Prices for tups range from £40 to £3,000 with occasional tups attracting bids as high as £6,000. The average price of the tups sold by an individual breeder ranges from £50 to £900. From my discussions with breeders, commercial farmers and shepherds, there was general agreement on two points: first, individual tups fetching prices less than £800 were 'commercial' tups and those in excess of £1,200 were definitely top-class tups; and second, those breeders whose tups averaged more than £450 were usually among the clique of top breeders.

These certainly seem to be accurate assessments of the bidding patterns, particularly among the clique, which one participant described as the 'I'll buy yours and you buy mine strategy'. At the Lockerbie sales I attended in the 1980s and 1990s, about twenty tups fetched prices in excess of £1,500 and all were from breeders in the visiting circle and all were purchased by breeders from the clique or those wishing to enter it. About ten breeders attained averages in excess of £450, and again all were in the clique. The twelve tup sellers with the highest averages and highest priced tups and the buyers of the ten to twelve most expensive tups were from the visiting circle.

The accuracy of participants' analysis of the bidding is not surprising because, as I described earlier, I was not the only one at the auction carefully taking notes. When all the tups from each breeder are sold, the average price is immediately calculated by those marking catalogues and a list is kept of the tups that receive the highest bids. Thus, throughout the auction, a kind of 'community of knowledge' about how each breeder is faring in relation to others spreads among all the participants, and by the end of the auction everyone knows whose tups have received the best prices and which breeders have the highest averages.

Community-making in circulation and redistribution of tups

There are several comments to make about the patterns of bidding for developing a sense of community around tups and sheep farming in the Scottish Borders. The bidding strategies in the Lockerbie auction are similar to the marriage strategies that in the anthropological literature are called direct exchange and circulating connubium and they have similar consequences for the participants' sense of community and place. I have already hinted at the essence of the strategy which breeders and commercial farmers alike recognize. The 'I'll buy yours and you buy mine strategy' is enhanced by breeders in the clique symmetrically offering very high prices for each others' tups 'so that *everyone* in the clique gets a reputation as a top breeder'.

I want to highlight two consequences of these bidding strategies for place-making a sense of community among hill sheep farmers. First, by *reciprocally* buying each other's best tups, members of the clique do not have to actually expend money for the tups because over several years they will spend on tups of other breeders what they receive from other breeders who buy their tups. Some members even organize beforehand a direct exchange: two breeders agree to buy a specific tup from the other for the same price. Although there are not the identified trading partners, the overall effect is a kula-like ring with money and tups moving around the clique both within one auction and over several years of auctions. As tups and money circulate, at any one auction the fortunes of individual breeders fluctuate in relation to the others, with some breeder or breeders in the clique getting a low average and their best tup receiving lower than expected bids. But as long as they continue purchasing expensive tups, their fortunes and the prices of their tups improve in later years. Over time, then, nothing happens to the financial and social status of members in relation to each other. To put this another way, the result of this circulation was a pool of money and high-quality genes that constituted and reproduced both the clique of eminent breeders whose farms collectively defined the locality of hill sheep farming and the eminent tups that represented the core of their identity as hill sheep farming people in the Borders.

Second, breeders in the clique make money from the sale of their lesser quality tups to commercial farmers outside the clique. In this pattern of exchange, there is in effect a redistributive system. Money from commercial farmers flows into the clique and the expert knowledge and stockmanship of the breeders embodied in the genetic pool, that even their lesser quality tups benefited from, flows back into the flocks of the commercial farmers. In this sense, then, the core genetic pool of top breeders' tups that embodies their consummate hill sheep farming stock-manship infuses flocks of hill sheep farms generally in the Borders. This is why the annual Lockerbie sales are so important for creating a sense of community among hill sheep farmers in the Borders. It is a celebration of, and mechanism for, the best South Country Cheviot tups bred by Border hill sheep farmers to mediate a shared sense of attachment between hill sheep farming people, inclusive of both breeders and commercial farmers, and the Borders region.

Conclusion

In this chapter, I have proposed two rather modest ways in which hill sheep farmers in the Scottish Borders help us re-conceptualize the concept of community. First, despite and because of the processes of deterritorialization that have disturbed the taken-for-granted experience of the inextricability of community and place in Teviothead – what I have called a predicament of emplacement – this has not led to people abandoning their place-making and sense of community. As several others have recognized (Nadel-Klein 1991, Gupta and Ferguson 1997, Hastrup and Olwig 1997), the experience has made the importance of community as place more explicit and urgent. On this basis, I have suggested that one dimension of community is that it is a place-making process; and both the character of the process and the sense of community created depends upon the particular social-historical context in which it occurs. Thus, rather than trying to rethink a singular and universal concept of community as place-making, I have described the place-making of a regional sense of community of hill sheep farmers by hill sheep farmers in the Borders of Scotland during the 1980s and 1990s. Second, in contrast to those perspectives which emphasize the importance of the boundary in constituting community, I have shown that it is the core of what it means to be a hill sheep farmer – embodied and represented by hill sheep – that is emphasized in their community-making.

Notes

1 Alverez concurs with this inverse relation between the experience of being-in-place and efforts at place-making: 'Whereas at one time we conceptualized culture as territorially contained units and communities as likewise bounded entities, we now attempt to reconceptualize these notions from the perspective of a deterritorialized world, a world in which cultural and ethnic identities have in turn become deterritorialized and yet, stronger' (1995: 449).

2 I have argued in another article (Gray 1998) that privileging the boundaries of concepts and phenomena tends to be of more concern in analytic practices of scholars than in the everyday practices of people in living their lives. The difference between the two modes of concept formation that I am describing here is similar to Burling's distinction between trying to define colour concepts in terms of drawing borders or selecting the focus, the 'truest' example, of each colour (1970: 46–49). Burling points out that this latter practice is more typical of the way people use colour concepts in everyday life. Daniel found a similar difference between how the Indian government defines a village in terms of cartographic boundaries and how Tamil villagers conceptualize it in terms of the important places that demarcate its spatial centre (1984: 74).

3 In this respect, I distinguish the way people in Teviothead talk about and experience community from the strategic use of the concept to refer to non-place-focused 'community of interest' – such as a set of people defined in terms of their professional activities (see Chaskin 1997: 521).

4 I include among the eleven tenants those farmers who occupied their farms under 'partnership' arrangements with the estates owning the farms (see Gray 2000).

5 See Gasson and Errington (1993) for an extended scholastic definition of a family farm business and Gray (1998) for a what I call a 'practical' definition.

6 Because the hilly topography, altitude, poor soil and climate are unsuitable for any type of agriculture except sheep farming, this region of Scotland has been categorized as a Less Favoured Area by the European Community. Farms in Less Favoured Areas are considered economically marginal and accordingly are eligible for special subsidies and headage payments that ensure their viability as businesses able to provide an acceptable standard of living for farming families and others living in rural communities (see Gray 1996).

7 A number of farms in Teviothead raised pure-bred Blackface sheep. However, this breed is farmed throughout Scotland. One of the major Blackface ram sales is held in the town of Lanark. Sheep farmers and shepherds from a wider area of Scotland than just the Borders region attend this auction. The origins of Blackface sheep are more in the highlands. Thus both the place where Blackface sheep originated and are farmed make them less exclusively a symbol of hill sheep farming in the Borders. For this reason, I base my account on the Lockerbie auction. Over several field trips since 1981, I attended the Cheviot Ram Sales at Lockerbie and the Blackface Ram Sales at Lanark. They were similar in most respects, though the sales at Lanark were much larger with over 2,300 rams sold and the prices were much higher.

8 I have adapted the title of this section from one in Geertz's ethnography of the Balinese cockfight (1975) in order to make a similar point. Like cocks for Balinese men, for border hill sheep farmers tups sold at the Lockerbie auction are highly valued, aesthetic objects that 'are symbolic expressions or magnifications of their owner's self' (1975: 419)

9 The term 'tup breeder' is applied to a farmer even if it is the farm's hired shepherds, like Charlie, who are 'tup crazy' and whose knowledge and skills are applied to raising, selecting and preparing them for the sales. Two of the tup-breeding farms in Teviothead fit into this category.

10 The prices quoted throughout this chapter are representative of the late 1980s and early 1990s sales. By 1996, there had been significant inflation in these prices so that highest price tups were between £2,000 and £10,000 and the highest averages were about £1,000.
11 There is no official reserve price set for each tup. Instead, prior to the sale of their tups breeders have to get a feel for the bidding to determine whether or not to accept the highest bid. The few tups that are 'passed in' (i.e. not sold because the owner did not accept the highest bid) are the ones that receive bids of less than £40. This seems to be the level at which criticism becomes insult – it is equivalent to what the animal would get at 'cast' tup sales where poor quality rams are sold for slaughter.

References

Alverez, R. R. 1995. The Mexican–US Border: The Making of an Anthropology of Borderlands. *Annual Review of Anthropology* 24: 447–470.

Anderson, B. 1983. *Imagined Communities: Reflections on the Origin and Spread of Nationalism.* London: Verso.

Anderson, J. L. 1986. *Profitability of Farming in South East Scotland 1984/85.* Edinburgh: The East of Scotland College of Agriculture, Agricultural Resource Management Department.

Appadurai, A. 1991. Global Ethnoscapes: Notes and Queries for a Transnational Anthropology. In R. G. Fox, ed. *Recapturing Anthropology: Working in the Present.* Santa Fe, New Mexico: School of American Research Press.

Auge, M. 1995. *Non-Places: Introduction to an Anthropology of Supermodernity.* London: Verso.

Basso, K. H. 1996. *Wisdom Sits in Places: Landscape and Language Among the Western Apache.* Albuquerque: University of New Mexico Press.

Blu, K. I. 1996. 'Where Do You Stay At?': Homeplace and Community among the Lumbee. In S. Feld and K. Basso, eds. *Senses of Place.* Santa Fe, New Mexico: School of American Research Press.

Burling, R. 1970. *Man's Many Voices: Language in Its Cultural Context.* New York: Holt, Rinehart and Winston.

Casey, E. S. 1996. How to Get From Space to Place in a Fairly Short Stretch of Time. In S. Feld and K. Basso, eds. *Senses of Place.* Santa Fe, New Mexico: School of American Research Press.

Chaskin, R. J. 1997. Perspectives on Neighborhood and Community: A Review of the Literature. *Social Service Review* 71(4): 521–554.

Cohen, A. P. 1982. Belonging: The Experience of Culture. In A. P. Cohen, ed. *Belonging: Identity and Social Organisation in British Rural Cultures.* Manchester: Manchester University Press.

Daniel, E. V. 1984. *Fluid Signs: Being a Person the Tamil Way.* Berkeley: University of California Press.

Flynn, D. K. 1997. 'We Are the Border': Identity, Exchange, and the State Along the Bénin-Nigeria Border. *American Ethnologist* 24(2): 311–330.

Gasson, R. and A. Errington. 1993. *The Farm Family Business.* Wallingford, UK: CAB International.

Geertz, C. 1975. Deep Play: Notes on the Balinese Cockfight. In C. Geertz: *The Interpretation of Cultures.* London: Hutchinson.

Gray, J. N. 1984. Lamb Auctions on the Borders. *European Journal of Sociology* 24: 54–82.

Gray, J. N. 1996. Cultivating Farm Life on the Borders: Scottish Hill Sheep Farms and the European Community. *Sociologia Ruralis* 36(1): 27–50.

Gray, J. N. 1998. Family Farms in the Scottish Borders: A Practical Definition by Hill Sheep Farmers. *Journal of Rural Studies* 14(3): 341–356.

Gray, J. N. 1999. Open Spaces and Dwelling Places: Being at Home on Hill Sheep Farms in the Scottish Borders. *American Ethnologist* 26(2).

Gray, J. N. 2000. *At Home in the Hills: Sense of Place in the Scottish Borders.* New York: Berghahn.

Gupta, A. and J. Ferguson. 1997. Beyond 'Culture': Space, Identity, and the Politics of Difference. In Gupta, A. and J. Ferguson, eds. *Culture, Power, Place: Explorations in Critical Anthropology.* Durham, North Carolina: Duke University Press.

Hastrup, K. and K. F. Olwig. 1997. Introduction. In K. F. Olwig and K. Hastrup, eds. *Siting culture: The Shifting Anthropological Object.* London: Routledge.

Herzfeld, M. 1991. *A Place in History: Social and Monumental Time in a Cretan Town.* Princeton: Princeton University Press.

Jackson, M. 1995. *At Home in the World.* Sydney: HarperCollins Publishers.

Jackson, M. 1996. Introduction: Phenomenology, Radical Empiricism, and Anthropological Critique. In M. Jackson, ed. *Things As They Are: New Directions in Phenomenological Anthropology.* Bloomington: Indiana University Press.

Nadel-Klein, J. 1991. Reweaving the Fringe: Localism, Tradition, and Representation in British Ethnography. *American Ethnologist* 18(3): 500–517.

Rapport, N. and A. Dawson. 1998. Home and Movement: A Polemic. In N. Rapport and A. Dawson, eds. *Migrants of Identity: Perceptions of Home in a World of Movement.* London: Berg.

Seamon, D. 1984. Heidegger's Notion of Dwelling and One Concrete Interpretation As Indicated By Hassan Fathy's *Architecture for the Poor.* In M. Richardson, ed. *Place: Experience and Symbol. Geoscience and Man,* vol. 24. Baton Rouge: Department of Geography and Anthropology, Louisiana State University.

Chapter 4

Cultural islands in the globalizing world

Community-cum-locality of the Cieszyn Silesian Lutherans[1]

Marian Kempny

Introductory remarks

It is common nowadays to maintain that the traditional anthropological confidence in the solidity of its analytical subjects, namely 'local cultures', 'isolated communities', or 'pure kinship structures' has recently been undermined. As my chapter is aimed at providing a closer look at the ways in which people nowadays construct the relationship between culture, community and place, this reconceptualization of the anthropological subject needs to be taken into account and subjected to further careful scrutiny.

It has often been taken for granted that social space constitutes a kind of neutral grid on which cultural differences are inscribed. Nevertheless, a recent wave of publications reveals that space seen from the anthropologist's point of view might be regarded as something contested and socially or politically created.[2] The idea of 'place making' as an answer to the fallacy of spatially deterritorialized notions of culture (cf. Gupta and Ferguson 1997: 6ff) draws our attention to the social practices in which community, locality and region are 'formed and lived'. As 'space is practiced place' – to quote Micheal de Certeau (1986: 117) – so cultural places are constructed rather than have much in common with discrete, object-like phenomena confined to discrete spaces (cf. Olwig and Hastrup 1997: 4).

In fact, it is necessary to distinguish between two basic aspects of the problem. On the one hand, the way of defining how culture and community are spatialized has to do with a broad conceptual framework through which one might think about the possible linkages between culture and place. On the other, 'cultures' and 'communities' are not only theorized or imagined, but lived through the daily reifications made by their members that persist despite the social scientists' claims about their decline.

As a result, the study of cultural forms in an age of alleged deterritorialization, creolization and hybridization heralded in the contemporary globalization discourse (cf. Hannerz 1992, Nederveen Pieterse 1995, Tomlinson 1999) requires a closer look at possible disjunctions of place, community and culture. However, in my opinion, instead of blindly following those theorists of globalization who a priori tend to conceptualize contemporary communities and their cultures as free floating, we should examine thoroughly the countless ways and contexts in which people themselves – sometimes deliberately and laboriously – may construct their places in particular social locations. This is why the empirical case will be made to show that the experience of deterritorialization of culture nowadays is frequently counterbalanced by self-reflexive efforts at an implicit mapping of 'localized cultures' onto definite places. Therefore, as I see it, it would be too hasty to conclude that community and culture can now be regarded as being totally devoid of any 'natural' relation to territory and to ridicule the conflation of community and locality as a totally naïve point of view.

Deterritorialization thesis and 'community' concept reexamined

One can argue that the endeavour to question the community/locality conflation precedes the recent globalization discourse. This argument is clear in an encyclopedic entry on 'community' by Nigel Rapport (1997: 114–117) that provides a succinct, but lucid account of the formation of this notion. Varieties of functionalism and structuralism – according to Rapport – were replaced by a symbolic approach most fruitfully applied by Anthony P. Cohen (1985). In turn, the previous reified notions gave way to a focus on how notions of community are given cultural meaning. Communities and their boundaries exist essentially as 'worlds of meaning in the minds of their members' (1985: 20). Therefore the community's 'essence' should be conceived as a kind of attachment to a common body of symbols, a shared vocabulary of values. As Cohen put it (1985: 20): '"Community" serves as a symbolic resource, repository and referent for a variety of identities and its "triumph" is to encompass these by a common symbolic boundary.' Consequently, resembling the notion of identity, the term 'community' might be basically regarded as contrastive: coupling closeness and sameness with distance and difference (cf. Rapport 1997: 115).

Such an approach is clearly heralded by the notion of 'imagined communities' coined by Benedict Anderson (1983). Although Anderson put forward this idea in the context of the origins of national communities, he maintained that ' all communities larger than primordial villages (and perhaps even these) are imagined' (1983: 15). It is noteworthy, however, that even though his conception implies a notion of 'community without propinquity', it does not undermine the significance of cultural constructions associated with place or landscape as concrete reference points that enable drawing the symbolic boundaries of community. It is rather that the national territory has been invested with a sort of surplus, symbolic meaning not reducible to its basic function as a locus of social relationships.

Undoubtedly, the process of globalization has enhanced our ability to imagine and create such 'deterritorialized communities' by radically redefining our experience of proximity and distance. The widespread discourse on so-called transnational communities must suffice here as an obvious example. Consequently, many students of current cultural trends put into question the view of community as consisting of a bounded group of people, resident in one locality, and culturally homogeneous. However, if one pushes such a stance to the utmost, it will leave us with the conclusion that communities are no longer anchored or moored to particular places and their members should be seen as eternally rootless and homeless.

To my mind, such a vision or diagnosis must be handled with care. First of all, widespread tensions and conflicts between different 'communities' (cultural groupings, minorities and the dominant group(s), etc.) generate demands for autonomy, which usually are expressed in terms of the symbolic making of spaces into particular places. Those discords over 'places' are often exacerbated by serious economic, political and social inequalities brought about by distant social forces and historical processes. Furthermore, in our world, social closeness and distance still tend to be articulated in spatial terms; territory itself often matters as a basis for community that sometimes is manifested by a process of 'remooring' the community concept itself as a part of 'demotic discourse' (cf. Baumann 1996).

Hence, one can argue that in order to recognize and understand the nature of the process of creation, re-creation, maintenance and change of communities – especially under globalized conditions – among a vast array of factors, such as tradition, social memory, mythology, prejudices and stereotypes, or wider ideologies, one must also include imaginings about the 'unproblematic', 'proper' places their members occupy. Thus, all this suggests the need for a conceptualization of community formation in spatial terms as a dynamic, creative process which may subvert globalizing tendencies construed merely as delocalization (Thompson 1995) or displacement (Giddens 1990).

My chapter thus offers an analysis of the developments in some localities in Poland which suggest the lasting significance of spatial reifications as a means of community reconstructing. The central concern of this chapter is, then, with the uses a particular social grouping might still make of its symbolically apprehended community-cum-locality in order to defend its status as an isolated, or rather a self-consciously created 'insular, island-like culture'. Under such circumstances, the term 'community' still serves as a framework accounting for localism conceived in terms of the embeddedness, encapsulation and social distinctiveness of one's own group.[3]

As T. H. Eriksen put it in much more universal terms:

> [t]he self-conscious, reflexive production of cultural islands has many similar features all over the world. The 'artificial' islands resemble one another more than the 'natural' islands they seek to replace. They are mediated by the interfaces of markets, states and seamless, global systems of communication. However, they manifest themselves only through an infinitive number of unique local expressions. Some of the differences between societies may be accounted for through recourse to explanations which reject the idea that human agency is important in the constitution of society. Some of them, however, are demonstrably created by humans who insist on their right to retain – and worship – their sense of living in an island.
>
> (Eriksen 1993a: 145)

Perhaps, what is peculiar to our own time consists in the enhanced significance of place as community boundaries become more and more vulnerable. Since the contemporary world does not allow for isolation, it is important to study the ways in which people reject the imposition of blurred identities by upholding such spatial reifications as the metaphor just mentioned.

In other words, the community nowadays turns from a 'given', a matter-of-fact part of local landscapes into an uncertain stake in the contestations over place and the continuing efforts of individuals to create their distinct collectivities. Hence, a specific research problem to be dealt with in what follows is the description of how recent pressures on community boundaries might be counterbalanced by diverse efforts to emphasize its inner coherence and separateness. This intricate issue will be taken up in the empirical context of the more or less reflexive, self-conscious attempts of 'Catholic sea islanders', namely the Cieszyn Silesian Lutherans, to keep their community alive during the arduous time of cultural change and political transition that Poland has been currently experiencing.[4]

The community of the Cieszyn Lutherans – past and present

Consequently, following Gupta and Ferguson's footsteps (Gupta and Ferguson 1997: 17), I will try to disclose 'how place making involves a play of differences' in the process of which identities (also spatial ones) are both overdetermined by structural location and open to contestation and restructuring.

Such a focus on the drawing of symbolic boundaries that bear upon cultural politics associated with a particular community requires a closer scrutiny of the historical context and the wider system of ethnic, political and economic relations within which place is constructed. Poland is widely known as a stronghold of the Roman Catholic Church, and that's undoubtedly true; however, there are parts of Poland where other denominations not only exist, but outnumber the Catholic population at the local level. The presence of Lutherans in the region of Cieszyn (Teschen) Silesia substantiates this claim.[5]

Cieszyn Silesia is a typical Central European borderland, historically and geographically connected with both Poland and Bohemia, as well as with the Austrian Empire. The region, despite the Polish ethnie (cf. Panic 1994), remained from 1327 in vassalage of the Bohemian Crown only finally to come under the reign of the Habsburgs of Austria in 1526.[6]

Traditionally, the main cause of differentiation among the mixed and internally diversified population of this region was religion. Nevertheless, a careful look at historical circumstances is needed in order to explain the wide spread of Lutherans in this area. Protestant confessions set up their diasporas in Poland soon after the beginning of the Reformation (i.e. when in 1517 Luther's theses were posted at the door of the Wittenberg Castle church). Yet, the dissemination of their beliefs was hampered by the royal restriction on freedom of faith.

In the Cieszyn Dukedom, in contrast, the reigning family initially promoted the impact of Martin Luther's teaching. Especially in the first half of the sixteenth century, the Dukes of Cieszyn supported the Lutheran faith and this movement got the upper hand over Catholicism among vast circles of locals. As a result, in the second half of the sixteenth century the population in this region was predominantly Lutheran (cf. Kubica-Heller 1996: 29ff. and Mach 1993: 225). However, after the Seven Years' War in 1763, when almost the whole of Silesia was taken over by Prussia, the Cieszyn region remained with Austria until the end of World War I.

The Counter-Reformation policy of the Habsburgs in this region led to the persecution of non-Catholic denominations. Lutheran churches were closed down and Protestant services prohibited. Lutherans found themselves forced to convert to Catholicism. It was not until 1861 that these pressures stopped, thanks to the granting of equal rights and religious freedom to the Lutherans following the promulgation of the Imperial Protestant Warrant issued that year. In the wake of the long period of oppression, the proportion of Lutherans fell; however, due to the uneven territorial distribution of believers, at the turn of the nineteenth century some communities still continued to be predominantly Lutheran.

This religious–confessional line of division ran parallel to divisions based on national (ethnic) identification. The Lutheran communities tended to speak a Cieszyn Silesian dialect related to Polish, while the Czech language was spread mainly among the Catholic population.[7] Additionally, the political dominance exerted by the Roman Catholic rulers of Austrian nationality generated profound strife between the 'native' Poles who tried to preserve their Protestant religion and the Catholic 'strangers'.

One can claim in this context that it is clearly resistance against both political and cultural domination that fostered the development of a particular collective identity among the members of the mostly Polish Lutheran communities in the Cieszyn Silesia region. One of the primary frames of reference for identity formation arose from belonging to a well-defined territorial site.

Their own homeland was perceived by the Cieszyn Silesian Lutherans as stretched out within the historical borders of the former Dukedom of Cieszyn. The Czechs and Germans were regarded as strangers who were separated by a clear language boundary and by religion. Contrary to the situation in the rest of Poland, in this region to be a Catholic often meant to be foreign, while Lutherans were usually Poles.

Needless to say, the questions of local (territorial), ethnic, national and religious identity in Cieszyn Silesia have been almost incessantly politicized, as in all border regions. This was especially clear at the twilight of the Austrian Empire at the beginning of the twentieth century. To put it briefly, the existing patterns of identity construction reflected discord among the rules governing religious identity, localism and nationality.

Whereas the Cieszyn Lutherans were bound closely to their Lutheran churches as a defence against religious coercion, at the same time other aspects of belonging defined them as natives – 'Cieszyn Silesians'.[8] And finally, these identifications interfered with their Polishness as an idea of belonging to the 'imagined community' of the Polish nation promoted at the turn of the century by nationalist activists born and bred in the region.

The end of World War I brought about the independence of Poland after 123 years of partition. It also resulted, however, in a fifty–fifty division of the historical region of Cieszyn Silesia into Polish and Czech parts. This division undermined the existing organic community of the Cieszyn Lutherans, and subsequently national identification ceased to be a decisive factor in the process of identity construction. Almost all of the Czechs lived on the other side of the border, while the German-speaking population remained mostly on the Polish side and had to coexist with the Polish majority.[9]

In the Polish part religion very soon regained its priority as the most important aspect of identity. This was especially the case since, due to the uneven distribution of the Lutheran population, there were whole communities in rural areas which were inhabited mainly by Lutherans.[10] Finally, in inter-war Poland, where the Roman Catholic Church enjoyed a privileged position, the main reference point for identity-shaping among the Cieszyn Lutherans was their minority situation *vis-à-vis* the dominant majority. What especially deserves to be mentioned is that inflamed conflicts cropped up at that time as a result of attempts to depreciate the significance of the contribution made by the Lutherans to the preservation of Polishness during the several centuries of foreign rule over the Silesian ethnie. The equation of the Lutheran faith with being a German, which was put forward by the Catholic clergy and some political ideologists and endorsed by the majority of Poles, strengthened the tendency of the Lutherans to isolate themselves in the form of a confessional community confined within a locality that kept apart from the Catholic inhabitants of the region.

In the memoirs of Jan Wantuła, the bishop of the Polish Evangelical Church of Augsburg Confession, to which almost the whole Lutheran population of Cieszyn Silesia belonged, it was expressed thus: 'At the very borderland, each Lutheran is a Pole, whereas each Catholic is a Czech' (ms., p. 79; quoted after Kubica-Heller 1996: 53). This belief nowadays still belongs to the familiar stock of knowledge at hand among Cieszyn Silesian Lutherans and is used in their struggle against the assertion equating Polishness with Catholicism. At the same time it is put in doubt by leaders of Catholic communities; indeed, the latter now even tend to stress that: 'in the late nineteenth century only Paweł Stalmach and a handful of people connected with the journal *Gwiazdka Cieszyńska* stood for Poland, whereas the majority of Lutherans were in favour of Germany' (a comment of a Catholic informant).

This isolation was especially visible when they lived in closed, local communities based on religion, religious institutions and standardized ascriptions that proclaimed the ideology of endogamy. Such a situation is well-documented but its broader analysis is impossible in the confines of this chapter. The recent, thorough analyses of Grayna Kubica-Heller (1996; esp. chap. 5) convincingly demonstrates that the Lutheran communities were at that time characterized by a social organization that permeated all crucial aspects of both individual and social life. Institutionalization of religious practices, the feeling of being threatened from outside, the process of internal homogenization of their confessions, strong social control and an articulated socialization model resulted in generating feelings of belonging to the community of the Cieszyn Silesian Lutherans (cf. Kubica-Heller 1996: 72). This strong link between identity and place was sometimes reinforced by the fact that Lutherans and Catholics occupied discrete ritual spaces located within their separate parishes and cemeteries.

At the same time, despite such transparent, clear-cut boundaries, the main levels of social classification did not necessarily reflect an unambiguous inclusion/exclusion basis of confession. Rules of social inclusion were also defined by feelings of belonging, of being rooted in a place wider than a particular locality and inhabited by Cieszyn Silesians. Thus, one can venture a hypothesis that what happened there was the territorialization of the collective memory of Cieszyn Silesians. It is Anthony D. Smith that describes such a process and attributes it to the nation-building process. Smith (1999) has also used the term 'ethnoscape'[11] to stress the importance of 'the process of territorialization of historical memory' which consists in a collective envisioning of national 'sacred territories'. In the case of the Cieszyn Silesians as well, the formation of their regional entity seems to demonstrate the involvement of the same mechanism through which a specific territory becomes perceived as unique and indispensable to the members of a community (cf. Smith 1999: 16).

The shared historical past clearly must have effected the collective shaping of the image of the former separate region of Cieszyn Silesia. In particular, transmitted through social memory, the spatial referents of collective identities of Cieszyn Silesians forged representations of a sort of 'community without propinquity' confined within the boundaries inherited from the bygone times of the Cieszyn Dukedom. For such a case Smith reserves a term 'miniscapes', which describes the links between a local population to a region that is much more circumscribed than national territory (cf. Smith 1999: 16).

In other words, the difference of religion as a symbolic marker of cultural variety in the region clearly coincided with grounding the Cieszyn Lutheran community in the shared experience of vital links between their historically shaped place and a localized culture understood as the sense of territorial embeddedness of their 'proper' places. Under such circumstances, to define 'community' meant introducing localism as a decisive factor that defined both social loyalties and detachments by referring to personal bonds with the territory of imagined ancestral land. Consequently, one can maintain that if an imagined community of the Cieszyn Silesian Lutherans survived the territorial annihilation of the 'proper' place they had inhabited in the past, it was partly thanks to their commitment to the historically shaped territorial notion of Cieszyn Silesia as their 'homeland'.

Cieszyn Silesians come to terms with social and cultural transformations

The so-called socialist industrialization and urbanization that took place in Poland in the wake of post-World War II reconstruction has hardly ever been regarded as connected with globalization because it ended up having only a very local impact. However, it should be kept in mind that these processes did bear upon a total disruption of territorial ties and that this justifies the use of a language of deterritorialization, in the fundamental sense of literal population displacement as an outcome of labour migration. Like many other areas of Poland in the 1960s and 1970s, the Cieszyn Silesia region became mostly a site of more literal than metaphorical movement and encounter. Yet, the spatial consequences of these flows has not been an ambivalence typical of an 'interstitial zone of displacement and de-territorialization' (Gupta and Ferguson 1992: 18).

As in the postwar years, the permeability of space tended to vastly increase in Poland and it might have resulted in a fragmentation of localized, religiously based communities and in a drastic reduction of the importance of the locality factor as a frame for identity formation. Nonetheless, it is my basic claim that despite all of these tendencies, local identity continued to play an important role as a dividing factor in the Cieszyn Silesia region and has regained its real importance in the recent period of radical social and political change. Furthermore, I am going to argue that the nature and significance of imagined connections with a particular place both lived in or left behind due to the new shapes of the political borders has been decisive for the way Cieszyn Silesian Lutherans now construe their 'island' in a Catholic sea.

It is probably true that under globalized conditions the experience of belonging is often tainted by ambiguity and indeterminacy. At the same time, the case of Cieszyn Silesian Lutherans makes clear that a sense of membership in one's community of origin still might frame experiences of spatial attachment and generate the basic forms of belonging. These forms are different from fixed social statuses and determine community boundaries by introducing the most radical ways of juxtaposing 'Us' and 'Them'.

Below, I will illustrate how a sense of the close ties between locality and community now finds its expression in the view held by Cieszyn Silesians of the relationship between belonging and place. It should also reveal how an intrusion of outsiders has strengthened the localism of the established, understood as a profound identification with a particular place, the bonds created by membership in various religious groups notwithstanding.

It is not to say that the communal ties among the Cieszyn Lutheran community did not undergo a notable transformation after World War II. As far as its territorial dimension is concerned, the reality of the new postwar world order in this region seemingly didn't lead to any spatial reconfiguration. Nevertheless, very important social and political processes took place in the communist era that had much to do with redefining a sense of attachment to specific places that constituted an important source of identity. First of all, under Communist rule strict control was exerted over the public articulation of 'identity' and religion was removed from the public domain. Consequently, the places of worship of the Cieszyn Silesian Lutherans became like a private territory, where people meet some familiar others in order to reconfirm their own ways of life rather then to affirm their distinctiveness *vis-à-vis* their Catholic environment. For instance, it is only the confirmation ceremony that still remains visible outside the confines of their churches.

At the same time, a tendency towards the lifting of the barely penetrable barrier separating the local Lutherans and Catholics was accelerated by the massive immigration of new Catholic inhabitants to this area.[12] Needless to say, this process led to a further plunge in the ratio of Lutheran inhabitants to Catholic ones.

As a result, the significance of the religious dimension has distinctly dropped in comparison with the relevance of the fact of embeddedness in the local realm, especially as far as marriage strategies are concerned (cf. Kubica-Heller 1996: 95ff.). A local Catholic spouse is nowadays more likely to be accepted than a newcomer recently settled in this region. Undoubtedly, such intermarriages have also undermined the previously unproblematic division of the religious space which, in part, fostered a disjuncture between Lutheran and Catholic sites.

This tendency has resonated with an evolution of mutual attitudes within both the Lutheran churches and the Catholic parishes in the region. A widely declared ecumenism that favours Christian unity has got the Cieszyn Silesians used to common worship and prayers and community-oriented cultural activities.[13] It has made the boundaries of ritual spaces blur so that even in the sacred domain, a previous impermeable division between the Cieszyn Silesian Lutherans and the Catholic inhabitants of the region has been definitely lost. All of this has resulted in a fading away of sharp differences, previously very conspicuous, as far as the collective identities of the Lutheran minority and the mainly Catholic milieu are concerned.

It has to be kept in mind, however, that because of the relational and contrastive nature of identity, collective identity is always a product of contact and conflict rather than isolation. Thus, the erosion of the boundaries of Lutheran community has not diminished the importance of the factors of territorial belonging and shared cultural legacy that gave rise to a sort of community encompassing the Cieszyn Silesia region. On the contrary, as soon as the Communist system collapsed both religion and local identity reemerged not only as vital elements of a new political landscape but as a kind of consciously applied procedure by means of which individuals attempt to classify themselves.

To put it in a succinct way, in the past it was possible for the Cieszyn Silesian Lutherans to define their identity on the basis of religion and nationality as embodied in their language and tradition. Later, religion intertwined with locality overtook the importance of national identification when Poland regained its independence as a nation-state. Nevertheless, it is the developments after World War II, most especially in the wake of the 1989 political breakthrough in Poland that really made a difference. To my mind, they staged a new basis for a Cieszyn Silesian Lutherans' community, which should be sought in a deepening commitment to 'place making'.

What seems to be a predicament for the student of the region is the very fact that a reemergence of a kind of confessional community here goes hand in hand with a wider process of territorialization of historical memory in which the reinvention of territorial integrity of the former Cieszyn Dukedom plays a crucial role. In fact, the very name – 'Cieszyn Dukedom' – is not much in use now. Nevertheless, the shared imaginings of the boundaries of this region are more or less coextensive with the territory of the former historical entity.

The significance of spatial markers of Cieszyn Silesians' 'imagined community' was one of the main interests during my fieldwork. Parenthetically, my observations find a strong confirmation in the findings of the recent studies carried out in the region by social geographers. Particularly telling are the results of a survey indicating that among inhabitants of this region, almost 95 per cent define themselves as Cieszyn Silesians and recognize themselves as inhabitants of a separate territorial entity (cf. Matykowski 1997). At the time of the research, the Polish part of this historical region had since 1975 been incorporated into the larger administrative structure of Bielsko-Biała wojewodship.[14] This structure was also perpetuated by the regional divisions introduced by the 'Solidarity' movement. Nevertheless, a territorial construct of the so-called region of Beskidy Highlands (*Podbeskidzie*) connected with these divisions has been, and is, contested in the area under study.

Moreover, the findings of social geographers also clearly demonstrated that the Cieszyn Silesia region is still mostly envisaged in a historical, territorial, transnationally extended form. If one recalls that the territorial integrity of the former Dukedom was seriously limited by the incorporation of this entity into the administrative grid of the Habsburg Empire after the death of the last member of the reigning dynasty more than 300 years ago and totally destroyed after World War I, it is remarkable that a large part of the region's population still recognizes as its important centres several towns now located in the Czech Republic, which have not belonged to Poland since 1919.

At the same time, the results of the survey proves the principal role of Cieszyn, traditionally identified as the 'capital' town of the region, as a dominant feature of these spatial representations. Almost 92 per cent of respondents regard Cieszyn as the capital of the region,[15] whereas only 7 per cent mention Bielsko-Biała in this role despite the fact that Bielsko-Biała (a former border town of the region) today dwarfs Cieszyn economically as well as in regard to the population size.

It seems that the work of collective memory, which is reflected in the above-mentioned findings, also animates the production of spatial representations of the Cieszyn Silesia region as a typical borderland. A memory of a convoluted history of the region, where the meeting of various religious, national, and cultural influences cumulated, both in cross-fertilization, and more often, turbulent clashes, makes it potentially an area of translocal contest or discord.[16]

Like many recent developments in inflammatory points spread all over the world, this case makes clear how frequently an often-heralded demise of territorial bonds turns out to be an illusion. The analysis of meanings the inhabitants of the region attach to particular places leaves only a small margin of negotiability while facing the persistent daily reifications concerned with places people think to be 'proper' for them. Again, Anthony D. Smith's argument with its emphasis on the naturalization of a community's history through 'poetic spaces' and 'sites of memory' seems to be particularly pertinent here.

In more general terms, seen in this light, the imagery of 'Cieszyn Silesia' as a bounded entity exposes both some features close to as well as some traits that cause it to diverge from 'the shifting world' of deterritorialized 'scapes' in which, allegedly, all of us live nowadays (cf. Appadurai 1991). The boundaries of the imagined world which the Cieszyn Silesians 'inhabit' are, in obvious ways, historically relatively arbitrary and only partly intersect with their own spatial locations, but at the same time, they appear to be scarcely negotiable or fluid.

A focus on the nature of Cieszyn Silesian localism should, then, enable us to disclose how the territorial reifications held by the Cieszyn Silesians reflect the enduring, intricate relationship between locality and community, which the processes of globalization put at risk. As defined above, the phenomenon of 'localism' is grounded in feelings of being rooted in a place, of experiencing a sense of continuity over time as part of a bounded entity. From this point of view, there are plenty of examples of local institutions involved in the creation of such feelings of supposed commonality and belonging. The most conspicuous are connected with public events and folk festivals.

As far as the element of celebration of localism is concerned, what might be regarded as their salient feature in the post-World War II period was a kind of conflation of national history and its local version. Since part of the Cieszyn Silesian homeland has been expanded out onto territory which, from their point of view had been lost to the former Czechoslovakia, a kind of ritual reintegration has become an element of place making.

In order to remake Cieszyn Silesia a kind of shared place of belonging, the permanent element of boundary-crossing was introduced. It was especially visible in Cieszyn itself where, for example, the May Day parades were usually connected with the uncontrolled crossing of the Czechoslovakia state border by the crowd of Polish participants in the marches. Needless to say, in an era of strict control of individual movement such acts of trespassing had to be approved and orchestrated by the municipality of the town.

Furthermore, the municipality also created public fora for events that had much in common with attempts at creating a local 'poetic space' or a 'site of memory'. Particularly important in this regard was the annual celebration of the anniversary of the erection of the town at the so-called Well of Three Brothers, a legendary meeting point of Cieszyn's founders. Briefly, the central motif of the legends is that the town was built at the meeting point of three brothers who had left their previous homeland to conquer and master the surrounding lands, and finally established the city in the place at which they met up after their toils. It is clear enough in this context that the communal myths of the foundation of the regional capital are supportive of an image of the transnational character of the region.

While all of these community commemorations have survived the 1989 developments in Central Europe, the prospect of the integration of Poland and the Czech Republic within European political structures has been strongly influencing the context in which they take place nowadays. As a result, it has brought about the obliteration of a 'quest for liberation' from 'Czech rule', until recently imbuing the regional ideology of Cieszyn Silesians.

As it is often expressed by them, the political boundaries of these nation-states are not meaningful as far as their territorial identities are concerned. In one of the responses to the question about the community that Cieszyn Silesians belong to, it is stated bluntly: 'Silesia, or properly speaking Cieszyn Silesia; now, when the state border is not any longer such a barrier as it was previously, people often think about the Cieszyn region in its historical boundaries'. What is noteworthy is that such attitudes of Cieszyn Silesians are fostered by a transnational economic integration and the total lifting of any restraints on the transborder movement of the inhabitants of this region.[17]

All this well illustrates the 'localized' nature of the community of Cieszyn Silesians. A tendency to rely on explicitly 'spatial' markers has continued to serve in this population as a factor which defines belonging, inclusion to, or exclusion from, a well-defined community of natives. A rather clear distinction between 'those who are rooted here' and the newcomers who are regarded as uprooted since they have arrived from 'Poland' today also encourages ascription either to the category of native born, *stela*, or to category of so-called *werbusy* (a derogatory label for guest-workers used by natives). These two different forms of belonging define the relation between 'Us' and 'Them', erasing the previous religious divisions.

In the same way, a gradual nature of belonging often emphasized by social anthropologists is denied here in the context of sharing the community's space. As described by one of the Cieszyn Silesians who has resided in Skoczów (a small town where my basic fieldwork was done) for a couple of decades:

> I'm not from 'here'! I stress it everywhere, I don't like to pretend that I represent the [Cieszyn] Silesian peoples. I'm not from here . . . Even when I was publishing an article in *Cieszyn Calendar* about my wife's grandfather I wrote about myself that it was written down by the husband of Mrs. Otylia Kocoń, who had come from 'Poland', as it's said here, from 'Poland'. Because I arrived from Poland.

A leitmotif of the interviews I have conducted resonates in the following statement by another inhabitant of Skoczów, in which the idea put forward eagerly by anthropologists that 'people can often be somewhat X' (Eriksen 1993b: 157) is implicitly played with:

> Obviously, there are divisions between those who arrived here some time ago and still are arriving and people who have been always living here, who are natives (*stela*). The most noticeable division is between [us] and the Osiedlowa street . . . This is the most specific neighborhood inhabited by the newcomers who somewhat got stuck there. They came there, live there, and I see it, it is there where the otherness is at its utmost.

This tendency towards assessing someone's personal identity in contrastive terms of belonging or not belonging, and of being the same or being different is also clearly visible among Cieszyn Silesian youth. While living their lives in the transcultural environment of a borderland and facing everyday flows of thousands of people crossing the national border, at least a part of the young generation seems to dream of belonging to a well-defined community of natives based on a shared tradition of the Cieszyn district as a separate territorial entity.[18] At the same time, youths brought up in the families of 'newcomers' tend to avoid stressing their links with this particular locality when defining their identities.

Consequently, one can come up with a tentative conclusion that the Cieszyn Silesian community still seems to be embedded in a spatial realm in which symbolic representations play a more significant role than the spatial locations of individuals and groups.

'Catholic sea islanders': what is 'place making' all about now?

As seen from the above, spatial perceptions based on shared experience coupled Lutherans and Catholic natives in envisaging the region as their common homeland. Nevertheless, though Lutherans and Catholics live there side-by-side, conjoined in their representations of the local universe, they remain separated by the deterritorialized boundaries of their religions. Moreover, despite the lack of distinctive features of particular social settings in terms of proximity and embeddedness of their members in a local realm, when looking now at the community of Cieszyn Silesian Lutherans, one can easily be attracted by the vocabulary of W. G. Sumner (1906) with his juxtaposition of 'we-groups' (in-groups) and 'they-groups' (out-groups).

Even in the face of the erosion of this community as a coherent grouping, it is mostly the same type of 'we-group' label that seems to phrase a dominant 'emic' model identifiable in, and widely shared by, Lutherans. In their feelings, however, the borders of their 'isolated island' go along with the regional ones that lead to an extension of their presumed shared ancestry to the Catholic natives and the exclusion of the in-comers.

One can try to interpret this apparent tension in terms of the contestations of the vision of 'territorial community' that came along with a dramatic change in the social context of Cieszyn Silesian Lutherans' collective life. Instead of territorially localized settings, the term has started to mean a construct developed by the natives close to 'localism', understood as a kind of immersion in a cultural site. What seems to be of crucial importance is that the collapse of real spatial boundaries, which formerly enabled the articulation of communal identities, has activated localism as a contextually contingent symbolic construction. Under these circumstances, the revival of the importance of religious identifications does not presuppose that religious 'embeddedness' is considered by the locals to be constitutive of the concept of the community.

At the same time, if one agrees that 'communities' and their boundaries exist essentially as symbolic representations 'in the minds of their members' (Cohen 1985), something important might be easily lost. It becomes especially clear as far as the notion of 'community-cum-locality' is concerned. No doubt, such an entity is based on the historically constructed perceptions of locality as well as grounded in the apparently immediate experience of belonging. However, as Gupta and Ferguson (1997) suggest, in order to understand how meanings of locality or region are formed, one must shift away from commonsensical, reified notions of locality or community towards a focus on social processes of place making.

Yet, these social and political processes should be 'conceived less as a matter of "ideas" than of embodied practices that shape identities and enable resistances' (Gupta and Ferguson 1997: 6). In this way, place making is not only a domain of the discursive framing of spatial imaginings nor has mainly to do with a direct sensory experience of proximity or belonging, but also with social practices that articulate 'the local' and transform it as well.

It is evident also that a reemergence of the previously invisible confessional community of Cieszyn Lutherans has happened thanks to the democratization process triggered off in 1989. When, due to political change, a suppressed religious identity has come to the fore, the process of lifting the boundaries of ritual religious spaces has been accompanied by a rhetoric of the 'isolated island', this time self-consciously adopted by Cieszyn Silesian Lutherans. To my mind, the obvious discrepancy between their representations of the 'insular' locality and the actual spatial locations of Cieszyn Silesian Lutherans cannot be properly accounted for without taking into account the broader cultural and political transformations in which this community is involved.

It may be disputable whether Cieszyn Silesian Lutherans could be regarded as an 'insular population'. At the same time, the dispersal of local communities coherent in religious terms that has taken place there is clearly counterbalanced now by a reenvisioning of the links between the Cieszyn Silesian Lutherans as members of the 'we-group' and 'their' land. Hence, as a by-product of the democratization process, the sense of a 'homeland' as a safe, domesticated space ('an island') opposed to the 'outside' world of 'out-groups' has been reproduced and enhanced within this group.

The symbolic boundaries of religion reflected in the opposition of the natives to the Polish-Catholic majority, predominantly bear nowadays upon the manifest techniques for solving the 'perennial problems' of living in a pluralist social environment (see e.g. Nash 1989). The whole specificity of these disjunctions consists of underscoring the significance of symbolic boundaries (also spatial ones) while striving for the recognition of group rights in different domains of public life (e.g. local governance, the school system, etc.).

The vibrancy of associational life is quite tangible nowadays and results in the expression of individual interests at a collective corporate level.[19] What should be stressed, however, is that numerous local cultural initiatives like the activities of the parish choirs, or folklorist events are aimed at the entire established population and thereby support a process of 'localization', which converts the Cieszyn Silesians into a regional community.

Furthermore, a consciously applied rhetoric of 'living in an island' does not prevent Cieszyn Silesian Lutherans from engaging in a variety of political or economic networks across a number of different spatial scales. Interaction across denominational lines invests social practices and institutional sites with the new meaning of community-cum-locality shared alike by Lutherans and Catholics of Cieszyn Silesia.[20]

This is not to say that there is no discord between Lutherans and Catholics rooted in the symbolic domain. The smouldering strife among the inhabitants of Skoczów, a small town of the region, might serve here as an example. It was triggered by the erection of a huge 'papal' cross on the top of a hill overshadowing the town. The cross commemorates one of the previous papal visits to Silesia and the mass connected with the canonization of Jan Sarkander which took place in Skoczów in May 1995. For a number of historical and doctrinal reasons, this canonization has been embroiled in many controversies and consequently, the cross itself is considered by some Lutherans to be a symbol of religious differences and the domination of the Catholic majority. In general, however, the analysis of local, both secular and religious, rituals (as cultural means which enable the construction of localism in different situations and the mobilization of the community to collective efforts) reveals that there is only a slight presence of symbolic conflicts between the Catholic and Lutheran inhabitants.[21]

However, it is worthwhile to mention that Lutherans place stress on the uniqueness of their 'insular' culture *vis-à-vis* the spatially distinctive group of presumed shared ancestry – the 'imagined community' of the Polish nation. As if deliberately engaging Weber's famous thesis about the link between Protestant ethics and the spirit of capitalism, many Cieszyn Silesian Lutherans seem to believe that their work ethic, efficiency and organization are superior to those of newcomers arriving from 'Poland'. They regard these virtues and assets as to some extent shared by the Catholic natives living in 'their island'.

End remarks: Locality as a project

I have so far referred to locality without any attempt at providing this term with some sort of analytical meaning. However, in order to sum up my considerations it seems, in the context of my own inquiry, propitious to probe into a technical use of the term introduced by Arjun Appadurai (1995).

The background for his reflection upon the production of locality was an on-going debate about the future of the nation-state in the wake of 'transnational destabilization'. Nevertheless, a distinction he introduces between 'locality' and 'neighbourhood' has general applicability and is of relevance for all types of community 'in a world where locality seems to have lost its ontological moorings' (Appadurai 1995: 204). According to his view, locality is 'primarily relational and contextual rather than . . . scalar or spatial' and, due to its 'complex phenomenological quality' (1995: 204), ceases to denote actual place, site, or locale. That is why, in his description, the key attribute of 'locality' becomes a structure of feeling which is produced by particular forms of intentional activity (1995: 208).

Appadurai also introduces another term, contrastive to 'locality': the notion of 'neighbourhood'. It describes 'the actually existing social forms in which locality, as a dimension or value, is variably realized' (ibid.). Therefore, this last term evidently serves as a replacement for a concept of territorial community unable to reveal the key features of human groupings in the contemporary world of global cultural flows. At the same time, 'neighbourhood', in Appadurai's view (1995: 223), shares only some properties assigned to this colloquial term like sociality, immediacy and reproducibility, whereas any expectations as to its size, sharp boundaries, or homogeneity are not implied.

One could easily agree that a wider sense of the term 'neighbourhood', which for Appadurai accommodates also an image of 'border zone', fits well as a description of the Cieszyn Silesian Lutherans moored in a collectivity that has lost its internal coherence and impermeable boundaries. Finally, then, by drawing upon the distinction Appadurai makes between locality as a universal property of social life and neighbourhoods as substantive social forms, I can try to recapitulate my argumentation in the following way: in the case of Cieszyn Silesian Lutherans, how is the relationship between locality and their neighbourhoods shaped at present?

Locality, as Appadurai defines it, is inherently fragile and must be continuously reasserted. The case of Cieszyn Silesians seems to confirm that in such a ceaseless process, 'the *spatial* production of locality' (Appadurai 1995: 205) still plays an important role. To my mind, what is really a significant modification concerns means of coping with the production of locality which have occurred along with a dramatic change in the social context of the Cieszyn Silesian Lutherans' collective life. Instead of territorially localized settings, the term has started to mean a construct developed by the natives which is close to 'localism' understood in terms of the sitedness of belonging. Consequently, despite the collapse of real spatial boundaries which formerly enabled the articulation of communal identities, locality as a contextually contingent symbolic construction has overtaken the importance of national, and subsequently religious frames of belonging, to the different 'imagined communities'.

Finally, the rhetoric of the 'isolated island' eagerly applied by the established inhabitants of the region confirms that localism has been replacing the religious basis of identity, forging a new unity in the community of the Cieszyn Silesians. In a globalizing world, cultural closeness and distance often tends to be articulated in spatial terms and 'space' still matters as a basic means for classifying and ordering the immediate social world. The same appears to be true in the case of Cieszyn Silesia, where localism is applied as a rhetorical strategy of reaffirmation and so provides those who live in a borderline zone of deterritorialization with a sense of continuity over the watershed of troubled times.

To conclude, while examining the extent of localization in Cieszyn Silesian Lutherans' neighbourhoods, the 'community' in all this appears not as an archaic form gradually disintegrating due to the erosion of its spatial basic, but as a shifting reality that is taking on new meanings. For quite a few Cieszyn Silesian Lutherans, a new basis is being sought in a deepening commitment to that which lies deeper than direct experience with the territory of the imaged ancestral land. It is the spatial imagery widely in use there which provides the ground on which new, transformed conceptions of community-cum-locality are made and re-made, again and again.

Notes

1 This work was supported by the Research Support Scheme of the OSI/HESP, Grant No.: 1323/1997
2 A critique of the extent to which anthropological thinking about spacialization of culture remains haunted by ideas of discrete, bounded, separate entities has been done recently by the contributors to several collections; cf. *Culture, Power, Space* (Gupta and Ferguson, eds 1997), *Locality and Belonging* (Lovell, ed. 1998) and *Siting Culture* (Olwig and Hastrup, eds 1997)

3 As one can imagine: 'localism conjures up several related images; being rooted in a place; the identity that comes from belonging; bounded social horizons; a sense of antiquity and continuity over time' (Strathern 1984: 185).

4 The empirical material discussed below comes from my intermittent fieldwork (1997–1999) conducted in this area. It should be emphasized, however, that results of the other field studies carried out in the Cieszyn Silesia region by Grazyna Kubica-Heller, Jan Kubick and Zdislaw Mach provide a useful background for my own analyses (cf. Kubica-Heller 1996; Kubik 1994; Mach 1993).

5 This region, which in its historical boundaries covered approximately 2,300 square kilometres (2,282 square kilometres), nowadays is divided by the state boundaries of Poland and the Czech Republic. Until very recently there was no territorial equivalent of the region in the grid of the administrative division of Poland. One can estimate the population inhabiting the Polish part of the former Dukedom at 165,000, of which 115,000 are Catholics and the rest the members of several other Christian denominations. The biggest of these is the Polish Evangelical Church of the Augsburg Confession with over 48,000 members in the Cieszyn Diocese (more than a half of the total number of its membership in Poland estimated on 85,000).

6 There was the separate Cieszyn Dukedom (*ducatus tessinensis*) during the time of the feudal disintegration in the late Middle Ages under the reign of the Silesian Piast dynasty (1290–1653), which later turned into a part of the Habsburg Empire.

7 The explanation one could come up with is that the Polish and Czech languages were the tongues of schooling and prayer for Lutherans and Catholics respectively. The maintenance of the Polish language among Lutherans was possible because the Lutheran schools had to be private ones which were allowed to decide about the language of instruction, whereas the Czech language was obligatory in public Catholic schools.

8 The ethnonym 'Cieszynioki' coined in the past is currently widely in use there.

9 When it happened, the population of the region in 1920 was 434,000, but of this number only 55 per cent were of Polish descent, 26 per cent Czech, and 16 per cent were of German nationality. Source: *Cesi a Polaci v minulosti,* Prague 1967, vol. 2. According to Zdzisław Mach (1993: 228), in 1923 the population of the whole region consisted of 76 per cent Poles and 23 per cent Germans (the remaining 1 per cent was of Jewish nationality).

10 It should be make clear, however, that in the 1920s the Lutheran inhabitants comprised only about 28 per cent of the whole population of Cieszyn Silesia, whereas among the village inhabitants they comprised *ca.* 35 per cent.

11 Interestingly enough, introducing such a usage of the term with an emphasis on the territorial base of a nation (or an *ethnie*), construed as 'a terrain invested with ethnic significance' (Smith 1999: 16), Smith seems to pay no attention to the fact that the notion 'ethnoscape' was invented by Arjun Appadurai (1991) in order to express a local element inherently present in cultural meanings produced in the contemporary globalizing world, where culturally created places of identification often don't coincide with the actual physical locations of their producers.

12 As elsewhere, this trend was triggered off by, and went hand-in-hand with, the urbanization and industrialization of the region. These changes caused, especially in the 1970s, a flood of newcomers, this time arriving mainly from very distant places in 'Poland', as the natives still tend to refer to the parts of the Polish state laying outside of Cieszyn Silesia.

13 It is noteworthy that there are often overlaps of regional, national and secular dimensions in these events. For example, festivals of church choirs or Christmas carol singing coexist smoothly with ecumenical prayers that are held to commemorate various local and national holidays.

14 The territorial reform introduced in Poland in 1999 that brought back a three-tier structure of self-government has finally reestablished a partial integrity of the former Dukedom under the shape of the district of Cieszyn (*powiat cieszyński*).

15 The town itself has been sharing the fate of the region which has been divided since 1919 into Polish and Czech parts.

16 The bloody and full of atrocities Polish–Czech border war of 1919 was a materialization of the explosive potential of disagreement about the boundaries of the region.

17 It has yielded an animation of the large-scale transborder petit-commodity trade localized mainly in the Polish part of the region, as well as in more 'global' initiatives like the establishment of a transnational institution of regional cultural and economic cooperation called 'Cieszyn Silesia Euroregion'. The very name of the 'Euroregion' reflects concerted efforts by the self-governments of the Polish and Czech borderline districts to strengthen bottom-up support by making use of an image from the past.

18 This thesis finds strong support in the light of materials gathered as the outcome of a literary competition for high-school youths on the subject of "To be a Cieszyn Silesian – does it still mean something?" (materials deposited in Macierz Ziemii Cieszyńskiej Library – Cieszyn).

19 For instance, the reactivation of the Lutheran Society in Cieszyn was caused by the attempt to set up a Lutheran high school (Liceum Towarzystwa Ewangielickiego) and this undertaking succeeded five years ago.

20 This is clearly seen in the domain of local politics. Swimming against the tide of national-level politics marked by a right-wing slogan – 'to be a Pole means to be a Catholic' – the local politicians have carefully avoided the risk of the conflation of political and religious divisions. Moreover, they formed local 'ecumenical' alliances that were able to win municipal elections in the two most important towns of the region in 1994 (their success was partially repeated in the 1988 municipal election).

21 To the contrary, the Cieszyn Lutherans have adopted some Catholic rites, like lighting candles on All Souls' Day (cf. Mach 1993: 230).

References

Anderson, Benedict (1983) *Imagined Communities*, London and New York: Verso.

Appadurai, A. (1991) 'Global Ethnoscapes: Notes and Queries for a Transnational Anthropology' in R. Fox (ed.) *Recapturing Anthropology: Working in the Present*, Santa Fe, NM: School of American Research Press.

—— (1995) 'The Production of Locality' in R. Fardon (ed.) *Counterworks: Managing the Diversity of Knowledge*, London: Routledge.

Barth, Fredrik (1969) 'Introduction' in F. Barth (ed.) *Ethnic Groups and Boundaries: The Social Organization of Cultural Difference*, London: George Allen & Unwin.

Baumann, Gerd (1996) *Contesting Culture*, Cambridge: Cambridge University Press.

Cohen, Anthony P. (1985) *The Symbolic Construction of Community*, Chichester and London: Ellis Harwood Ltd & Tavistock Publications Ltd.

De Certeau, M. (1986) *The Practice of Everyday Life*, Berkeley: University of California Press.

Eriksen, T. H. (1993a) 'In Which Sense do Cultural Islands Exist?', *Social Anthropology* 1, 1B: 133–147.

—— (1993b) *Ethnicity and Nationalism*, London: Pluto Press.

Friedman, J. (1994) *Cultural Identity and Global Process*, London: Sage.

Giddens, Anthony (1990) *The Consequences of Modernity*, Cambridge: Polity.

Gupta, Akhil and Ferguson, James (1992) 'Beyond "Culture": Space, Identity and the Politics of Difference', *Cultural Anthropology* 7,1: 6–23.

—— (eds) (1997) *Culture, Power, Place: Explorations in Critical Anthropology*, Durham, NC: Duke University Press.

Hannerz, Ulf (1992) *Cultural Complexity: Studies in the Social Organization of Meaning*, New York: Columbia University Press.

Kubica-Heller, G. (1996) *Luteranie na Śląsku Cieszyńskim*, Bielsko-Biała: Głos Życia.

Kubik, J. (1994) 'The Role of Decentralization and Cultural Revival in Post-Communist Transformations: The case of Cieszyn Silesia, Poland', *Communist and Post-Communist Studies* 27(4): 331–355.

Lovell, Nadia (ed.) (1998) *Locality and Belonging*, London and New York: Routledge.

Mach, Zdzisław (1993) *Symbols, Conflict, and Identity: Essays in Political Anthropology*, Albany: State University of New York Press.

Matykowski, R. (1997) 'Śląsk Cieszyński a Podbeskidzie. Świadomość regionalna mieszkańców województwa bielskiego (spojrzenie geograficzne)' in I. Bukowska-Floreńska (ed.) *Śląsk Cieszyński i inne pogranicza w badaniach nad tożasamością etniczną, narodową i regionalną*, Katowice: Silesia University Press.

Nash, M. (1989) *The Cauldron of Ethnicity in the Modern World*, Chicago and London: University of Chicago Press.

Nederveen Pieterse, Jan (1995), 'Globalisation as Hybridization' in M. Featherstone, S. Lash, R. Robertson (eds) *Global Modernities*, London: Sage.

Olwig, Karen Fog and Hastrup, Kirsten (eds) (1997) *Siting Culture: The Shifting Anthropological Object*, London and New York: Routledge.

Panic, I. (1994) 'Przyczynek do problemu świadomości narodowej mieszkańców Księstwa Cieszyńskiego od Średniowiecza do początków reformacji' in T.

Lewowicki (ed.), *Poczucie tożsamości narodowej młodzieży. Studium z pogranicza polsko-czeskiego,* Cieszyn: Uniwersytet Śląski – Filia w Cieszynie.

Rapport, N. (1997) 'Community' in A. Bernard and J. Spencer (eds) *Encyclopaedic Dictionary of Social and Cultural Anthropology,* London and New York: Routledge

Redfield, R. (1960) *The Little Community and Peasant Society and Culture,* Chicago: Chicago University Press.

Robertson, R (1995) 'Globalization', in M. Featherstone, S. Lash, R. Robertson (eds) *Global Modernities,* London: Sage.

Smith, A. D. (1999) 'Secret Territories and National Conflict', *Israel Affairs* 5,4: 13–31.

Strathern, M. (1984) 'The Social Meanings of Localism' in T. Bradley and P. Lowe (eds) *Locality and Rurality: Economy and Society in Rural Regions,* Norwich: Geo-Books.

Sumner, W. G. (1906) *Folkways: A Study of the Sociological Importance of Usages, Manners, Customs, Mores, and Morals,* Boston, MA: Ginn.

Thompson, John B. (1995) *The Media and Modernity,* Cambridge: Polity Press.

Tomlinson, John (1999) *Globalization and Culture,* Cambridge: Polity Press.

Chapter 5

Community beyond place
Adoptive families in Norway

Signe Howell

I

In the beginning I almost burst with pride every time I bought a tin of baby food. Everyone could see that I was one of them; someone to be reckoned with. I had become someone who was a part of the community (*fellesskapet*).

(Norwegian adoptive mother in conversation)

II

I think that these children are ours to a greater extent than if we had given birth to them ourselves. We have given them a country, a language, a family. In a sense we have given them life itself.

(Letter from an adoptive mother to the journal published by an adoption agency)

III

I thought it was idiotic [to attend]. Mum said it was OK that I did not go, but then I would have to come up with a good reason for not going. That was really daft. I could not think of a good reason so I had to go. I kept thinking 'what am I doing here?' We did not have anything in common. I just looked at them. Some of them were really dark-skinned.

(Adolescent adopted girl about a social gathering of transnationally adopted children organized by one of the adoption agencies, in Brottveit 1999: 47)

These statements by two Norwegian adoptive mothers of children from Columbia and Korea respectively and a transnationally adopted adolescent girl, express very succinctly the paradoxes inherent in transnational adoption. They show what I wish to call the adoptive family's dilemma, namely the desire for conformity and the having to admit to non-conformity. Conformity in the case of parents is focused entirely upon the wish of couples to become 'normal families' and their inability to achieve this in the usual biological reproductive manner. While, on the one hand, they want to be part of the ordinary community in which they live and, in a sense, are able to feel this as the first statement indicates, their part in this larger community is achieved only through being members of a sub-group, namely that made up of other adoptive families. Conformity in the case of adopted children is expressed in the majority's wish not to be thought of as different, and the efforts they engage in in order not to stand out, but live as ordinary Norwegian children and adults. The paradox here arises when we consider that most of them do not look like native-born Norwegians.

In this chapter I wish to pursue these people's realities and argue that a sense of belonging is vital for human satisfaction. It is, however, possible to belong to many different communities and according to different criteria of belonging. My argument will be that, whereas a large proportion of the adoptive parents establish a sense of community amongst themselves, the majority of adopted children do not. Place becomes one important marker of belonging, but it is not by any means the only one, nor necessarily the most important. Moreover, I shall argue that looks need not be a major determining factor when it comes to inclusion or exclusion, but rather cultural attitudes to the significance of looks. This raises questions of degrees of experience of being outsiders and the motivations for belonging, as well as attitudes at large in the dominant society. A related aspect, which I cannot deal with here, is the degree to which exclusion from, or inclusion in, a collectivity may ultimately be regarded as a question of power – not least a power to define the operative criteria in any given setting.

Many critical voices have been raised in recent years against attempts at talking about collectivities – not to mention culture and society. It is suggested instead that we talk in terms of agents and agency, choice, flux, multiplicity of meanings (e.g., Borowsky 1994). However no-one, to my knowledge, has yet argued against the proposition that human beings in their very essence are social beings. Recent work on child development (e.g. Bråten 1998; Trevarthen and Logotheti 1989) has demonstrated that within hours of birth, babies strive to engage in meaningful communication with the significant others that surround them; in other words, they are competent social partners from birth. From this, they argue, it is reasonable to assume that human beings construct meaning intersubjectively. Both (or more) parties jointly engage in meaning-making in a two-way process. From such a perspective, understanding about the world in which one lives is not uniform, but dependent upon the actual series of communications all of us engage in. At the same time, communication is not idiosyncratic, but, to borrow a phrase from the literary critic Stanley Fish, actively relates itself to an 'interpretative community' which 'declares (in its preoccupations) what is and is not literature at any given time'. Thus, Fish rejects objective and realistic description in favour of interpretation, but embeds the interpretation in social conventions rather than in idiosyncratic subjectivity (Fish 1980: ch. 1). These insights inform my approach to an examination of the construction of possible communities amongst Norwegian adoptive families and adoptees.

As Cohen pointed out more than fifteen years ago, in order to be meaningful domains of interaction, communities need boundaries. The word 'community' both marks that the members have something in common and that this commonality distinguishes one community from another. 'Community thus seems to imply simultaneously both similarity and difference. The word thus expresses a *relational* idea . . . Indeed it will be argued that the use of the word is only occasioned by the desire or need to express such a distinction' (Cohen 1985: 12). Like Barth (1969) and others before him, Cohen is interested in demonstrating that much of what is analytically interesting happens at the boundaries between groups because it is at the boundaries individuals may exercise their choice. What goes on inside the boundaries became for these writers less interesting. While activities and manipulations of criteria at boundaries may be revealing about deeper concerns and constraints, and hence the analytic focus on the significance of interactions on and across boundaries certainly has proved fruitful, it is in my view only part of the story. Certainly, Cohen's demonstration of the symbolic construction of communities went a long way to remedy the disdain expressed by Barth against an interpretative interest in the 'cultural stuff' that occurs within the boundaries (Barth 1969). But surely it is of interest to turn the argument round and say that just as boundaries create distinction, they may equally create unity, conformity, and a sense of belonging within the boundaries. There are real challenges attendant upon examining these senses of belonging analytically and theoretically.

It is precisely 'the cultural stuff' that seems to me to be of interest when we study the construction, and expression, of something we might meaningfully name communities. What has become clear in recent years, however, primarily through the work of Anderson (1983) in his discussions about so-called 'imagined communities', and the more recent work on Diaspora and transnational movements (e.g. Olwig and Hastrup

1999; Gupta and Ferguson 1997; Rapport and Dawson 1998), is that place, or location, need not be an integral part of a sense of community.[1] Given an analytic acceptance of community's divorce from locality, it becomes even more important to try to identify what the cultural stuff consists of in each case. In this chapter I will consider three different possible communities, each from the point of view of Norwegian adoptive parents and/or their adopted children. Each community carries different connotations and employs different criteria for inclusion (and exclusion), but each is constituted relationally according to a set of criteria that establish interlocutors as 'one of us' and 'not one of us'. For community to be a valid socio-cultural category, I shall argue that its members have to agree on some shared reality and also, somehow, to be recognized by others as actually being a community. This mutual acceptance is a result of a negotiated understanding and need not be absolute. From the point of view of adoptive families, several groups may be relevant as communities for them. They can be listed as follows:

1   Norwegian society at large, as demonstrated by the first quote above.
2   The special quality of being an adoptive family within the larger Norwegian community, as demonstrated by the second quote.
3   The adopted children themselves may potentially constitute a separate community within the larger Norwegian community. The third quote will be examined from such a perspective.

In what follows I will try to elicit how the different participants develop – or not, as the case may be – discursive practices which in each case are, according to my argumentation, developed intersubjectively. What is important is to discern how values and practices in society at large are reflected both amongst those categories of people who directly affect the adoption process (psychologists, social workers, agency personnel, bureaucrats) and those directly concerned, namely the families.

Transnational adoption in Norway

The 1950s in Norway was a period of establishing the welfare state along social democratic principles. It was a time when, politically, the housewife was idealized as the role model for women and the family its natural counterpart (Frønes et al. 1990: 26; Gullestad 1997). Family life based on the nuclear family living in its own house and slowly accumulating new consumer goods became the aspiration of the majority. Those who failed to conform through involuntary childlessness could easily feel marginal to the preoccupations of society at large.

Due to a rapid decline in Norwegian-born babies and infants being made available for adoption,[2] the practice of transnational adoption started in the late 1960s in Norway. Since then, there has been a steady and rising demand to adopt children transnationally. Between 500 and 600 babies and infants arrive each year (most are under 3 years of age upon arrival) making Norway the largest recipient *per capita* of adopted children. Children come from about twenty different countries in Asia and Latin America. The vast majority have come, and continue to come, from South Korea and Columbia, with China rapidly gaining in popularity. During the past decade, children have also arrived from Russia and other eastern European countries and from Ethiopia. Today, approximately 16,000 adopted children have been integrated into Norwegian families. What these figures mean is that more than one per cent of the annual birth rate is made up by transnationally adopted children. In light of the improved methods of assisted conception, the figure, perhaps surprisingly, shows no sign of declining. The practice is so common that most adult Norwegians will have some personal knowledge of children being adopted from overseas. Most likely a relative, a friend or a neighbour have created their family based on one or more children adopted from overseas. Although there are larger clusters of adoptees in the Oslo region and some other parts of the country, they can be found throughout the whole country, both in urban and rural areas. Recent studies on the development and adjustment of the adoptees show that the vast majority are well integrated into Norwegian society and they have performed as well as, or even slightly better than, the national norm in terms of education and employment (Botvar 1999, Brottveit 1999, Sætersdal and Dalen 1999).

In this chapter I shall not examine the fate of the adoptees, but rather the conflicting scenarios that are available to them as members of non-biologically constituted families and the strategies that the parents employ in order to cope with the numerous ambiguities and paradoxes that arise during the families' life histories. I wish to argue that the parents display a creative approach to handling these ambiguities and that they continually reinterpret and elaborate on their experiences and their situation according to context and purpose. Indeed, I have argued elsewhere (Howell 2001) that when it comes to the most profound dilemma of all, namely the understanding of the meaning of kinship as biological or sociological, they alternate between foregrounding and backgrounding the one at the expense of the other, according to the demands of the particular discourse and context. They do so, I argue, by creating cognitive boundaries between the available explanatory models, and the contradictions apparent to the observer are ignored by they themselves. When it comes to the process of kinning (Howell 1999) their children, incorporating them into their own kin network as well as into Norwegian society, biological sources of kinship are backgrounded. In the context of the community of adoptive families, biological facts of kinship may be foregrounded. Whether this makes them active agents in charge of their particular fortune – as so many contemporary theoreticians advocate that people everywhere are (e.g. Gupta and Ferguson 1997; Olwig and Hastrup 1997); or just pragmatic managers of their own realities engaged in continuous intersubjective creation of meanings with those significant others who occupy the same reality, I do not wish to consider here. My interest lies more in exploring the ways in which the adoptive parents work at connecting their children with different communities, and how they create possibilities for them to belong to them. I also wish to explore the various criteria for belonging that are marshalled in the different cases, and the resultant ambivalence that arise out of such a project.

Despite my argument that anchored and shared place – or locality – need not be a constituent feature of a community as was previously held to be the case by anthropologists, the idea, or rather the value, of place nevertheless features in all the discourses that I have examined. While communities in many cases consist of people linked through a particular locality, they may also consist of spatially and socially dispersed people who nevertheless regard themselves as profoundly related, but through shared experiences and symbols rather than localities. It is striking that in my material on families made up of Norwegian parents and transnationally adopted children, a sense of community exists between the parents regardless of where they live in Norway, or whether they ever actually meet one another. Strong empathy exists between adoptive parents regardless of personal relationship. Face-to-face interaction is thus not a necessary prerequisite for community to come into existence, for boundaries to be drawn around a perceived shared specialness. However, one important criterion, but not the only one for constructing a community of relations in addition to the fact of having adopted a child transnationally, is nevertheless based on significant places that they share a connection to. For example, the common country of origin of their children, the common orphanage, or more abstractly the fact of having visited their child's place of origin, all become significant localities that strengthen the feeling of being connected. I also wish to suggest that the strong emotional feeling of relatedness that converts adoptive parents into a community would not have come about had it not been for the fact that they have all engaged in close face-to-face interrelationships with some other adoptive parents at various stages of the process. The strong bonds of empathy would be established not only through membership in the associations and the literature, but is achieved through sharing the same experiences together. I return to all these point below.

The value of localizing identity

Let me return to Anderson's by now almost cliché observation, but no less insightful for that, that face-to-face relations linked to a locality are not a prerequisite for a sense of community. Using the ethnographic example taken from Indonesia, a multi-ethnic, multi-cultural nation-state if there ever was one, he shows that a sense of 'imagined community' is established through a set of common symbols (1983).

While the notion of boundary also features in Anderson's study of an emerging Indonesian sense of nationalism, he is more concerned with explicating the symbols that made this possible. In line with this approach, I turn now to an examination of, first, what some of the significant elements are that make up the 'cultural stuff' which provides Norwegians with a sense of community, and second, what elements provide the adoptive parents with their special sense of community within the larger Norwegian one. I conclude with an open-ended question of why the majority of adopted children fail to develop a corresponding sense of community.

Most writers agree that a place of origin features strongly in most Norwegians' understanding of self and identity (Kramer 1984; Gullestad 1999). If one regards kinship as a 'primary regime of subjectivation' (Faubion unpublished manuscript; Howell 1999) as a means of plotting, and of being plotted into, a life trajectory in relationships with significant others, then I will argue that in the Norwegian case, such plotting cannot occur without some reference to place of origin. Urbanization only took off in Norway after World War II and many writers (Larsen 1984; Witoszek 1998) argue that most Norwegians are still country folk at heart. Certainly, to be able to trace one's ancestry to a valley, a fjord, a remote district of some kind, and preferably to an old farm there, is highly valued by Norwegians. Not to be able to name a locality steeped in kinned history can be felt as a distinct loss. This attachment to locality is expressed most graphically in the local version of a national costume (*bunad*). There are more than twenty different *bunad* styles, each explicitly linked to a locality and, strictly speaking, one should not wear one that cannot be traced to a kinned connection to the locality. Such *bunad* are very popular and a large proportion of the female population (men wear them less frequently) possesses one. They are worn on the national day and on important public or private occasions. Those clad in the same *bunad* interact in a familiar manner even though they have never met each other before. This is noticeable on big public occasions when total strangers can be seen to approach each other because they wear a *bunad* from the same district.

It seems to be very important for adoptive parents to emplot their adopted children's trajectories in conformity with their own places of origin as soon as they arrive in Norway. Through a number of different measures, they engage in a kinning (cf. Howell 1999) process of the child, that is incorporating it into their own lineages. One common method is to 'plant' their children in the soil of their ancestors (Howell 1999; 2001). A clear manifestation is seen in the photographs that parents have to include in their progress reports to the orphanage from which the child came. Frequently, the photographs include a scene from the family farm, and/or the holiday cottage in the region of one parent's or (grandparents') place of origin. Certainly, photographs of the child together with grandparents, aunts and uncles and cousins are invariable included. A pride and pleasure in the natural environment is frequently mentioned as an integral part of Norwegian identity. Many photographs of the adopted children are taken in natural settings – never to my knowledge in urban ones. Finally, the children are very often dressed in a national costume that traces its heritage to either parent's place of origin. From these facts one may conclude that belonging to a locality is important in adult Norwegians' formation of self.

It is also important for adult Norwegians to interact as a couple with other couples – whether married or not is less important since cohabiting has become a national norm. According to my material, involuntary infertile couples who opt for adoption want children in order to 'become a normal family'.[3] I have argued elsewhere (2001) that the desire for children is a desire to be able to practise family life in interaction with other couples of the same age group – most of whom have children. Daily and social life for people between the ages of 25 and 45 in contemporary Norway is largely centred around activities that involve children. Between 91 per cent and 94 per cent of women will have given birth by the time they are 40 years old (Noack and Østby 1981; Sundby and Schei 1996). The present and the previous governments have continuously improved the provisions for birth leave and for families with small children, drawing the fathers more actively into the caring role of fathers. Those who fail to produce children tend to feel cut off from the wider social world around them. Many feel disengaged from society more generally. They do not feel that they have a stake in the political, economic, and social developments that are taking place, and they miss this. The first quote at the beginning of this chapter demonstrates the joy of being part of the collectivity on equal terms with the rest. The equal terms are here construed as being a mother (or father) of a small child engaging in activities that mothers (or fathers) usually do. Adoptive parents emulate what they perceive as typical family life. Indeed, they are in some respects more 'normal' than 'the normal ones', taking great care to engage actively in ordinary family activities and making sure their children also do so. Thus they make a deliberate bid to be accepted and included in what they regard as quintessential Norwegian social and cultural life. It is worth noting that not only does Norway score highest on transnational adoption, it is also at the top as regards the percentage of women actually giving birth. The two facts are hardly accidental. Thus, from all sides an emphasis on family, on motherhood and fatherhood, on belonging and normality are discernible. Ultimately, it might arguably be said that the very notion of 'Norwegianness', the community of 'true' Norwegians, which these days are challenged by the increasing number of immigrants, finds a collective rallying point through an enhanced public display of family life and belonging.

So far I have not contributed to a deconstruction of the concept of community. Rather, my study of Norwegian adoptive parents has strengthened the idea that national sentiments are constituted through shared symbols of place and locality grounded in kin associations. By continuing their preoccupation with kinned places and kinned sociality on behalf of their adopted children, they re-confirm, as it were, the norm whenever biology fails. Indeed, boundaries are created around notions and practices of Norwegianness in this case. Inclusion becomes dependent upon fulfilling these criteria. It becomes extremely difficult for immigrants to choose to manipulate the criteria and move across the boundaries for their own benefit – especially those who belong to a different religion, adhere to different principles of kinship and sociality, and who look different from the average Norwegian. There are very few openings for strategic manipulations of the boundaries between native Norwegians and such immigrants. The transnationally adopted children, on the other hand, are, in most cases, successfully led across them by their parents. To illustrate this point, let me briefly mention an incident that took place last year in Oslo.

Norwegian National Day is celebrated by the whole population throughout the country in a festive manner. Norwegian flags fly from every flagpole, public amusements are arranged in each locality. The climax of the day is the procession of children that winds its way through every town and village in the country. The children wave Norwegian flags and sing national songs accompanied by brass bands. *Bunads* from every district are much in evidence. Women allocated some official task are usually dressed in a *bunad*. In Oslo, the procession is made up of children from more than 100 schools, each with its brass band. It culminates at the royal palace, where the royal family waves to the cheering crowd. In 1999, for the first time ever, an immigrant, a Pakistani woman with Norwegian citizenship, was appointed to be the leader of the preparatory committee and to lead the procession. She was one of three immigrant members elected to Oslo City Council. About 20 per cent of the current population of Oslo is made up of immigrants or the children of immigrants from the South or from Eastern Europe, a fact which in many circles is construed as a major problem. Her appointment caused much public debate. She even received death threats. Since the woman had no kinned connections to a Norwegian rural locality, she had no right to wear a *bunad* on this occasion, as a native Norwegian in the same position would have done. Adopted children, on the other hand, as stated above, are clad in a *bunad* almost immediately upon arrival in the country, and it is accepted that they are.

The example demonstrates that a distinction is made between various categories of immigrants from the South. On the one hand there are those who are adopted into a Norwegian family and who are not defined in common parlance as immigrants.[4] They become integrated in the kinship system of their adoptive parents and think of themselves as Norwegian (see below). On the other hand there are those who remain outside Norwegian kinned relationships and who tend to gather together according to country of origin. They are perceived as immigrants and remain on the outside. Thus, it is possible for non-native born Norwegians to cross ethnic boundaries and to become incorporated into the native Norwegian community. This is achieved only on the initiative of the majority group and by a sleight-of-hand denial of differences. More importantly, connectedness is achieved within an idiom of kinship.

Despite the multiple realities lived by actual native Norwegians, the *idea* of communality of values and discursive practices shared in by all Norwegians does exist. This is clearly expressed in the self-presentation of both prospective and recent adoptive parents. An examination of application forms to the adoption agencies reveals a remarkable conformity amongst the applicants. Despite different places of origin, occupation, and background, they all emerge as very 'normal', or rather they conform to standard media notions of typical Norwegians. In order to be accepted by the authorities as suitable parent material most have worked out for themselves what the cultural norms and dominant values in contemporary Norway are and have chosen to conform as closely to these as possible. This was confirmed when I examined the reports and photos parents send to the donor orphanage once a child has arrived. Although there are few class or regional differentials, there are clear gender stereotypes. In the application forms women claim to like home-making, gardening, and handicrafts and the men to like fishing and pottering around with engines. Almost universally, both claim to like outdoor life. Hardly anyone lists artistic or literary interests; certainly not urban ones. This picture confirms those who argue that nature is part of culture in Norwegians' understanding of themselves and what it means to be Norwegian (Witoszek 1998). Despite the individual preferences and practices that clearly must exist in these people's lives, an imagined Norwegianness nevertheless has its own reality, expressed in an excess of banalities. So far, no immigrant couple has approached the adoption agencies seeking to adopt. It would be interesting to see how they choose to present themselves once they put forward claims.

Communities of shared experience

I turn next to a consideration of the more unfamiliar constitution of community which takes place between families who have adopted children from overseas. Within this community, place and locality of origin cease to be important for establishing community feeling, as does genealogical or biological kin-grounded relationships. The meaning of sociality amongst adoptive couples is predicated upon one common feature only, namely the fact of adoption itself. Despite all their avowals that they are 'normal' families, adoptive parents cannot altogether avoid facing the fact that, in some profound ways, there is a limit to their normality; their children are not their biological children. The most obvious indicator of this is the fact that the children look quite different from their parents. In the days when only Norwegian-born children were adopted, it was possible to pretend that the child was one's own biological child. The situation today makes this impossible. One consequence of this is that while, through adoption, adoptive parents achieve their longed for aim of becoming a family with all that seems to entail, their bodies consistently deny the normality of the family. This creates one common bond between adoptive parents. Another common bond is the painful experience of infertility. Upon learning about their infertility, several years usually pass before a couple decides to adopt. With an increased expertise in new reproductive technology during the past decade, in recent years most infertile couples have gone through one or more attempts of assisted conception. Having once decided to adopt, however, it takes, on average, another three years before they can bring their new child 'home', as runs the jargon in the adoption circles. The emotional stress that these couples undergo is clearly very different from that experienced by those who give birth without undue difficulties. Almost all adoptive parents I have talked to insist that, although their family and friends were very supportive during this difficult time, only those who have gone through the same process themselves can appreciate what it means. Wanting and having children is among the most personal and intimate activities that humans engage in. When the process is entangled in strong cultural elaborations and evaluations for both husband and wife, as is the case in contemporary Norway, it arouses strong emotions.

Through their various activities the adoption agencies[5] contribute to creating a sense of community between their members. Several different, but interrelated fora exist that encourage the practice of sociality between the adoptive couples and families which both mark them off as different from other Norwegian families and bond them together. Participating while they are waiting to be allocated a child in one of the preparatory courses on parenthood with a transnationally adopted child, which are arranged throughout the country, couples form close bonds that may last a very long time. It is common for such groups to continue to meet long after their children have arrived. They maintain an active interest in each other's triumphs and tribulations. These groups tend to be locally or regionally based. Other couples meet each other when they travel to collect their children. In some cases, the parents must wait several weeks before they have completed all the formalities and can take the child home. During such periods of shared intense emotionality, profound bonds are often forged. It is not uncommon to hear such couples refer to each other as 'almost family'.

A number of sub-groups have been formed which serve to emphasize the common situation of the adoptive families. These may be based on country of origin or just on the fact of having adopted transnationally. The Indian, Columbian, Ethiopian associations and so on organize regular get-togethers for families from all over Norway. People come from far away just in order to participate. The most commonly heard argument for making the effort is that it is so good for the children to keep in touch with other children like themselves. When the children are small, they are usually too young to realize the special quality of their families. When they get older most lose interest, as evidenced by the quote from the girl at the outset of this paper. It is my strong impression that rather than being good for the children to interact, it is good for the parents to do so.

I have argued elsewhere (Howell 2001) that although the families have nothing in common beyond the fact of adoption, at these gatherings a kind of meaningful past is jointly being constructed. This, in turn, helps the parents to make sense of the present and to face the future. It is a past that is made up of a shared experience of the liminal stages of abnormal pre-pregnancy, pregnancy and birth (Howell 2001) and what may also be called a shared liminal place. The place in question is linked to concrete places of origin that are outside of Norway and therefore not part of their own Norwegian kinned places of origin, but places which they, as adoptive families, have a share in. Such common places change according to the interlocutors. At the most general level, it is the fact of an alien country in itself that locate the families' origins outside that of the Norwegian locality and community. For those who have adopted from the same country, it becomes the country itself. More specifically, the shared place can become the town and the orphanage. It may also include the hotel or guesthouse where the parents stayed while waiting to complete the formalities. For this to work, it is not necessary that they were there at the same time, only that the places are identical. This hugely emotionally loaded space is filled with meaning by all concerned. Through repeated redescribing and reliving the time and the place, at the social gatherings they create a historical trajectory for themselves as families; a trajectory which makes up for the missing Norwegian one. Thereby, they make sense of their current family situation and normalize it. By doing it jointly with other families, they all create a semblance of common origins which take on semblances of kinship discourses. In other words, they create a community.

Such social gatherings are striking to the observer. The parents are tallish, blondish, and light-skinned whereas the children are shortish, dark-haired, and dark-skinned. Only when they are together as a group does such a family constitute the norm. All these parents have worked extremely hard at creating a family for themselves. Through giving time, effort, and love they have sought to transform their children into Norwegian children and provided the parameters for a life that the children come to regard as normal. From this perspective, the statement by the second mother quoted at the beginning of the paper to the effect that despite not having given birth to these children, the adoptive parents have given them (a) life makes sense. Indeed, they are supported in this belief by their children. As social beings constituted as kinned selves, the vast majority of children experience themselves first and foremost as Norwegian. Many will admit to some confusion about their own identity at certain stages of their growing up. 'I have a Norwegian mind and psyche in an Indian/Colombian/Korean and so on body' are common statements but, by and large, the evidence shows that most adjust relatively painlessly to Norwegian cultural values and practices (Botvar 1999; Brottveit 1999; Sætersdal and Dalen 1999). On occasions when they are gathered together only with other adoptive families, the fact of adoption is foregrounded at the expense of the normal Norwegian family scenario which operates at all other times. On these occasions, transnational adoption is in the centre of attention to the exclusion of other concerns and interests. This particular aspect of their lives is identical with all the others present, regardless of place of origin or of living, of education, work, interests, age or personality or any other qualities that usually bring people together in meaningful interaction.[6] At such moments, interaction is made meaningful solely on the basis of one fact: their non-biological children born by unknown parents in unknown places. However, because wanting, having, and bringing up children is such an intimate part of life, the inability to engage in this has been desperately grieved for by these parents. This fact encompasses all others and makes seemingly unlikely people establish profound relationships.

A more relaxed expression of connectedness can be observed on the so-called return visits, or motherland tours, which are organized for families with increasing frequency by the adoption agencies.[7] Ten to fifteen families with adolescent or adult adopted children travel together for a couple of weeks to the children's country of origin. During this trip they reaffirm the special quality of their families. The focus during the visit is on the country as a tourist attraction and on places connected to the children's past before they came to their families. I have argued elsewhere that attitudes to the country are that of rather superficial tourists where 'culture' consists of dress, food, and standard tourist attractions; what I call a folkloristic approach (Howell 2001). This, of course, contributes to maintain a distance to the country for all concerned. Despite an increasing tendency by the agencies to encourage the parents to instil a sense of pride in their children for their country of origin, they rarely delve below the surface of cultural tourism on these trips. Interestingly, the parents wish to identify places associated with the children before they came to them – the steps on which they were abandoned, the orphanage where they were looked after – but not to trace biological relatives. This is not to say that a shadow of biological origins does not hang over the whole enterprise. Nevertheless, it was my impression that a communal feeling within the families and between similar families is reinforced on such trips. The children rarely experience a sense of belonging to their country of origin as a result of such trips. Rather, more often than not, their Norwegianness is confirmed. They commonly feel distant from the local population despite the fact that, for the first time, their bodies conform to the norm around them.

Although the sense of community that I argue exists between adoptive parents is not dependent upon face-to-face interaction and therefore may be characterized as an imagined community, the various clear vehicles for communication which are derived in all cases from some analogous personal experience are vital for establishing a sense of community, of collectivity. The agencies are instrumental in this. Since all applicants have to be members of one of the three adoption agencies in order to be allocated a child, they receive the publications put out by the agencies and are strongly encouraged to participate in the various activities organized throughout the country. This fosters a sense of community. Prospective and adoptive parents read articles about others who have gone through the same process as themselves and about topics that are of interest to all adoptive families more generally. This, coupled with first-hand experience of some interaction of subsets of adoptive parents, means that they are able to empathize with those many others about whom they read, but of whom they have no personal knowledge. It might be argued that without this interaction to draw on, a category of collectivity is likely to remain a conceptual category rather than, as is the case, become a community. It seems likely that some sort of social intimacy, particularly when this takes place at vulnerable times, must occur to serve as a paradigmatic vehicle for the wider sense of shared experience.[8]

The boundaries that define the community of adoptive parents, unlike those that define Norwegian society, are rigid. Criteria for inclusion are clear-cut and absolute. However, the values, the meanings, the practices attributed in the discourse of transnational adoption are not exclusively worked out inside the boundaries. They are also the product of public debates and discourses in Norway, in other Western recipient countries, and in the various donor countries. Intersubjective processes of communication are conducted across all sorts of boundaries. Those issues which pertain to aspects of procreation and reproduction, children, families and family life, and to the fact of transnational adoption that, for whatever reason, do not resonate, are filtered out.

The adoptees

Reigning paradigms in British and American psychological circles who concern themselves with adoption and fostering hold that it is better for non-white children to be brought up in non-white families, or rather in families whose genetic make-up in racial terms matches their own (e.g. Triseliotis 1973; Brodzinsky 1990). In these models one may discern an implicit supposition that an authentic, or acknowledged, ethnic identity must coincide with genetic origins and bodily characteristics (see also Brottveit 1999: ch. 4). In much of this thinking, which is reflected in legal provisions in Britain and the USA as well as amongst social workers and others engaged with adoption, one may discern a kind of analytic collapse between genetics on the one hand and ethnicity or culture on the other. I return to this below. Interestingly, these ideas have only partially been incorporated into Norwegian public thinking on transracial adoption. Rather, as I have shown, the emphasis here goes in the opposite direction, namely to ignore the differences and transform the children into Norwegian children. This is probably due to a lack of children of any racial group available for adoption inside Norway. However, ambiguities exist. Traces of similar notions about race and ethnicity can be found in recent elaborations on the significance of roots, and of the desirability of establishing meaningful relations with the country of origin. Arguably, such notions can be said to constitute the *raison d'être* for return visits, for the distribution of cultural artefacts to the adoptive families, as well as the admonishment to the parents to 'instil in their children a sense of pride in their country of origin'. The question remains to what extent such theories are applicable to the adopted children's own experiences and priorities.

In the autumn of 1997 an organization calling itself *Network of Transnational Adoptees in Norway* (NUAN) was formed. Its purpose was to provide a forum for young people between the ages of 18 and 25. At its first general meeting, about 140 young people from the whole country attended. To some extent, the idea had been initiated by two of the adoption agencies and they were instrumental in making it happen by giving financial support to the conference.[9] The stated aim of the organization is to provide a common forum and, whenever necessary, support for the transnationally adopted young people. A forum to discuss common experiences, share thoughts, anxieties and so on. In Sweden a similar organization had been started a couple of years earlier and had attracted a large membership. It is curious therefore to note that the same did not happen in Norway. When the second annual meeting took place a year later only about twenty-five people attended. The membership is not growing. In March 2000 there were about eighty members. Given that several thousand transnationally adopted people within the age group live in Norway, it seems fair to conclude from this that Norwegian transnationally adopted young people do not feel that they constitute a community. While the parents do give such an impression, their children do not. The fact of being adopted does not represent a sufficiently important characteristic of their self-perception for them to actively engage with other adopted young people. This is clearly brought out in the third quote listed at the outset of this paper. If transnational adoption itself does not constitute a sufficient criterion for communality, the country of origin might. Several adoptees have told me that they feel some common bonds with those who originate from the same country as themselves, more than they do with the transnationally adopted generally. To my knowledge, two such organizations exist, one for people adopted from Korea, the other for people from Columbia. They distribute information about the countries, give classes in local cookery, and, from time to time, language courses. Depending on the leadership at any given time, the associations may be active. But even at its most active, their membership represents only a small percentage of the potential.

What is clear from mine and others' studies on the transnationally adopted people is that, in most cases, they are not much concerned about the reality or otherwise of their kinned relationship with their adoptive parents and other relatives. While some may at times of adolescent turbulence shout to their adoptive mother that 'you are not my real mother', such reactions do not suffice as a basis for a shared communal feeling with other adoptees. Research has shown that the adopted children are well integrated into their local community – at least as long as they continue to live there. A kind of colour-blindness operates amongst their friends and neighbours, and they are fully accepted by all as the son/daughter of farmer Jones or whoever. Most adoptive parents succeed in incorporating their children into their own social and kinned community.

In so far as ethnic boundaries are drawn in contemporary Norway, the native Norwegian category includes transnationally adopted children, but excludes immigrants and their children. As the adoptees leave home, they may come across strangers who assume that they are outside the Norwegian cultural reality that they themselves think they belong to (Sætersdal and Dalen 1999). This is felt as a shock by the people themselves. Most adopted children I have met insist that they are not immigrants. Almost all the adoptive parents interviewed in a recent study expressed anxiety about their children's future in terms of racism. Their main concern is that casual strangers would not distinguish between their children who 'really are Norwegian' and the children of immigrants (Brottveit 1996: 133).

With a few exceptions, the adoptees are very anxious not to be defined as immigrants and actively resist being included in that category. As far as they are concerned, the boundaries that separate immigrants from Norwegians are clear-cut. They have few problems with defining themselves as belonging inside the Norwegian group. Indeed, some may express more hostility towards immigrants than do their parents or native Norwegian peers. So, far from feeling bonds with these other 'new' Norwegians, they deliberately distance themselves from them. Far from feeling an ethnic solidarity, they feel an ethnic 'role-handicap' (Brottveit 1999: 91). They resent being asked by strangers where they come from. More interestingly, perhaps, is that these feelings of resentment do not lead to a feeling of solidarity with others like themselves.

The pedagogues Dalen and Sætersdal, who for more than fifteen years have been studying the development of identity in a group of adoptees from Vietnam and India, and more recently Columbia, confirm these findings. What seems to be that case is that by far the largest majority do not identify themselves with their country of origin and with people who come from that country. They argue, however, that transnationally adopted people in Norway may be described as 'a new cultural category in Norwegian society' (Sætersdal and Dalen 1999: ch. 10). This is argued on the basis of what they call their 'double-marginality'. Their status as adopted and their status as having a different ethnic origin from their adoptive parents mean that they are neither Norwegian nor immigrants (ibid.: 156). While I see the temptation of such an argument, I cannot agree with it, except at a rather trivial level. First, the concept of 'double marginality' implies that the adoptees are doubly outside Norwegian society, a fact my material contradicts. Second, what might be meant by 'cultural category' is highly problematic and not discussed. Third, such a category is externally imposed. It is not, as I have argued, confirmed by those who are allocated to it. As discussed at the outset, for any social, cultural or ethnic category to exist analytically, it must exist empirically in the sense that it is acknowledged as such by its members and, ideally but not necessarily, attributed a status by outsiders. In the case of transnationally adopted people, it would be difficult to find arguments that establish any of these criteria If, minimally, community has to exist in the minds of its members (Cohen 1985: 98), then there is no community of transnationally adopted people in Norway, although there is one amongst their parents. It has to be remembered that the parents are already firmly inside the Norwegian community (although as infertile couples they felt peripheral in important aspects) and thus feel secure in that regard, whereas their transnationally adopted children occupy a more ambivalent position.

In order to be convincing about the reality of a community, I would argue that one needs to demonstrate the existence of shared experiences, shared emotions, and shared symbols. Other factors, such as shared locality or place, face-to-face interactions over time, are neither necessary nor sufficient, but may at times prove highly significant. Communities must be generated from within and somehow be set apart. Regarding actual membership, this is determined in each case through criteria for inclusion or exclusion. Whether or not one may cross boundaries will remain an empirical, not a theoretical question.

Notes

1 One has perhaps dismissed the relevance of place too easily. Most Diaspora are linked *inter alia* to a shared place of origin or belonging. Thus Jews in Oslo, New York, and Sarajevo all constitute their Jewishness on the Holy Land. Palestinians throughout the world similarly talk in terms of the 'homeland', and the struggle to reclaim this legitimizes the struggle.

2 The decline in unwanted pregnancies can be attributed to the decline in the social stigma of single mothers, the financial support extended to single mothers, free contraception, and abortion on demand.

3 Despite the prevalance of unmarried couples, Norwegian regulations have until 1999 insisted that applicants for adoption be married. What often happens amongst other couples is that once they have a child, they get married.

4 Adopted children do, in fact, appear on the annual national demographic statistics as immigrants. This is thought of as very provocative by their parents.

5 There are three licensed non-profit making adoption agencies in Norway that between them bring about 600 children to waiting couples each year. It is they who have contacts with orphanages in the various countries and who match a child with a couple. They also engage in many extra-mural activities such as arranging parenthood courses for waiting adoptive parents, subsequent courses on adoption and puberty, and arrange discussion groups, seminars, etc. for their members. They publish journals in which articles from various experts (psychologists, social workers, and medical doctors) debate issues of relevance to adoption, as well as letters from members with

news of their families. They also organize family tours to the country of origin, operate an advisory service for members, and help children who wish to seek their 'roots'.

6 On these occasions a nod is made in the direction of the alien places of the children's origin. Food from the various countries may be served and cultural artefacts may be on sale in order to raise money for aid projects in the donor country.

7 I participated in one such trip to South Korea in 1999.

8 This point was made by Vered Amit as the editor to this volume. I had failed to make the connection and am grateful to her for pointing it out to me.

9 This further demonstrates the active part played by the agencies in shaping attitudes.

References

Anderson, B. 1983 *Imagined Communities: Reflections on the origin and spread of nationalism*. London: Verso.

Barth, F. 1969 'Introduction', *Ethnic Groups and Boundaries*, ed. F. Barth. Oslo: Norwegian University Press.

Borofsky, R. (1994) *Assessing Cultural Anthropology*. New York: McGraw-Hill.

Botvar, P. K. 1999 *Meget er forskjellig. men det er utenpå—? Unge utenlands-adoptertes levekår og livskvalitet*. Oslo: Diaforsk Nr. 2.

Brodzinsky, D. (ed.) 1990 *The Psychology of Adoption*. New York: Oxford University Press.

Brottveit, Å. 1999 *Jeg vil ikke skille meg ut! Identitetsutvikling, ekstern kategoris-ering og etnisk identitet hos utenlandsadopterte fra Columbia og Korea*. Oslo: Diaforsk Nr. 4.

—— 1996 '"Rasisimen" og de utenlandsadopterte. Norsk nyrasisme og kultur-forståelse belyst ved erfaringer fra utenlandsadopsjon' *Norsk antropolgisk tidsskrift* 2, 1996.

Bråten, S. (ed.) 1998 *Intersubjective Communication and Emotion in Early Ontogony*. Cambridge: Cambridge University Press.

Cohen, A. P. 1985 (1993) *The Symbolic Construction of Community*. London: Routledge.

Fish, S. 1980 *Is There A Text In This Class?* Cambridge, MA.: Harvard University Press

Frønes, I. et al. 1990 *Childhood as a Social Phenomenon: National report, Norway*. Vienna: European Centre Childhood programme: *Eurosocial report* 36/1.

Gullestad, M. 1999 'Setting boundaries: Connections between discourses on childhood and the Norwegian "no" to the European Union'. In Å. Daun and S. Jansson (eds) *European Encounters: Essays on cultural diversity*. Lund: Nordic Academic Press.

—— 1997 'A passion for boundaries: Reflections on connections between the everyday life of children and discourses on the nation in contemporary Norway', *Childhood* 4(1) 1997: 19–42.

Gupta, A. and J. Ferguson (eds) 1997 *Culture, Power, Place: Explorations in critical anthropology*. Durham, NC: Duke University Press.

Howell, S. (1999) 'The kinning of selves: creating life trajectories in adoptive families' (unpublished). Paper prepared for the conference on *Kinship and Temporality* at Goldsmiths College, London.

—— (2001) Relative values: New directions in kinship studies. In S. Franklin, and S. Mckinnon (eds) *Relative Values: New directions in kinship studies*. Durham, NC: Duke University Press.

Kramer, J. 1984 'Norsk identitet – et produkt av underutvikling og stammetilhørighet'. In A. M. Klausen (ed.) *Den norske væremåten*. Oslo: Cappelen.

Larsen, T. 1984 'Bønder i byen – på jakt etter den norske konfigurasjonen'. In A. M. Klausen (ed.) *Den norske væremåten*. Oslo: Cappelen.

Noack, T. and L. Østby 1981 *Fruktbarhet blant norske kvinner. Resultater fra Fruktbarhetsundersøkelsen 1977*. Oslo: Statistisk Sentralbyrå (*Samfunnsøkonimiske studier* nr. 49).

Olwig, K. Fog and K. Hastrup (eds) 1997 *Siting Culture: The shifting anthropological object*. London: Routledge.

Rapport, N. and A. Dawson (eds) 1998 *Migrants of Identity: Perceptions of home in a world of movement*. Oxford: Berg.

Sundby, J. and B. Schei 1996 'Infertility in a sample of women agenda 40–42', *Acta Obstet. Gynecologica Scandinavia* 1996: 832–837.

Sætersdal. B. and M. Dalen 1999 *'Hvem er jeg?': Adopsjon, identitet, etnisitet*. Oslo: Akribe.

Trevarthern, C. and. K. Logotheti 1989 'Child in society and society in children: The nature of basic trust'. In. S. Howell and R. Willis (eds) *Societies at Peace: Anthropological perspectives*. London: Routledge.

Triseliotis, K. 1973 *In Search of Origins: The experience of adopted people*. London: Routledge & Kegan Paul.

Witoszek, N. 1998 *Norske Naturmytologier: Fra Edda til økofilosofi*. Oslo: Pax.

Chapter 6

'Have you been to Hayward Field?'

Children's sport and the construction of community in suburban Canada

Noel Dyck

Introduction

While the moral order of Canadian suburbs celebrates the ideal of 'family togetherness', their geographical expanse systematically frustrates the realization of this goal. The cost of suburban housing typically requires two incomes, with the logistical consequence of affording parents, who may well have to commute some distance to and from paid employment, with reduced time to spend with family. What is more, the rapid pace of movement into, and out of, the relatively new and growing suburbs of the Lower Mainland of British Columbia does little to promote or sustain extra-familial relationships between either children or adults. Yearning for a sense of community or belonging in such a setting reflects adults' and children's respective social positioning, but is further challenged by the characteristic impersonality of suburban living. 'Suburbanization' is, indeed, often stereotypically likened to a virtual disappearance of communal relations (Gusfield 1975: 96) or a retreat of social activities behind the closed doors of family life (Fine and Mechling 1991: 60). Pronounced social differentiation and dispersion do, in fact, engender forms of residential isolation that make extra-familial social life tenuous. Moreover, contemporary suburban life is frequently accompanied by gnawing parental insecurity about the adequacy of efforts at child rearing (Fine and Mechling 1991: 72–3; Dyck 2000a, 2000b). Hence, although the origins of suburbia may have celebrated a family-centred environment that declared the importance of providing for children within a domestic setting (Fishman 1987: 7–8) and that also implied the existence of community, in practice the exigencies of contemporary suburban life in British Columbia make the realization of these ideals a difficult matter. Nevertheless, suburban residents seek in differing ways and with varying degrees of success to fashion arrangements for overcoming isolation and connecting with others, not least through various renderings of community.

The concept of 'community' has a long and contested status in anthropology as in the social sciences in general (Amit, this volume; Gusfield 1975; Bellah et al. 1985; Cohen 1985, 1987; Rapport 1996). In addition to being a concept of 'always positive evaluation and evocation, whose usage expresses and elicits a social group and a social environment to which people would expect, advocate or wish to belong' (Rapport 1996: 117), academic treatments of community tend to underscore the precariousness of this form of association. Since the founding of sociology and anthropology as academic fields in the nineteenth century, there has been a continuing concern within both disciplines that community remains under threat of extinction from the unrelenting forces of industrialization, urbanization, and westernization. Thus, two essential sets of questions persistently resurface in the academic literature on community. First, is community possible, can it survive and, if so, how? Second, why bother to maintain community? What does it offer its members?

A preliminary and generic response to the latter question is that community is not merely a categorical affiliation, but a form (or set of forms) of association that entails substantial, if episodic, social content in the form of face-to-face social relationships. The assertion of various forms of community and the cultivation of membership in one rather than another community provides a means for people to exercise some degree of choice in and control over their lives. The other concern – how is community possible? – is addressed in Cohen's (1985, 1987) analyses of the symbolic construction of community. Cohen's exegesis of the symbolic dimensions of community focuses upon the flexibility that permits ostensibly shared symbols to be, and to mean, many things to many people.

'Community' remains an ambivalent part of the ideological tangle that underpins 'home' and 'family' in suburban settings (Richards 1990: 178–9). The tension that exists between maintaining an appropriate degree of home and family privacy while avoiding complete domestic isolation dictates a need for caution in organizing neighbouring relations. Since neighbours potentially pose the greatest danger to domestic privacy, a fine line needs to be maintained between 'being friends' and 'being friendly'. Friends are permitted and expected to know one another, but being a good neighbour depends upon strategically and diplomatically 'not knowing' much that might be readily observed (Richards 1990: 226–31). Beyond neighbouring relations and practices, however, lies the possibility of becoming 'involved in the community' through participation in one or another organized group. This chapter examines the use of organized sport for children and youth as a carefully monitored vehicle for child rearing that also serves as a malleable medium for constructing varied notions and experiences of community for adults and children in the suburbs of metropolitan British Columbia.

The ethnographic case study presented in this chapter directs our attention to several taken-for-granted assumptions concerning the expected, requisite nature and dynamics of community. Specifically, in documenting the bonds of affiliation that sometimes emerge as an outcome of participation in children's sport activities in suburban locales, I challenge the notion that a sense of belonging, identification with a social group or place making necessarily involves or requires wide-ranging, multiplex and enduring relationships. Instead, drawing upon ethnographic evidence, I suggest that relationships of community may be relatively narrowly circumscribed in time and space and decidedly partial or situational in content, and yet highly salient as means of affiliation. That these relationships may be restricted in range and episodic or even ephemeral in duration does not, however, mean that they are lightly felt or inconsequential. Parents and children involved in community sport activities may experience a deep sense of commitment to the athletic events and formal and informal relationships that comprise this realm of leisure. Accordingly, they may invest remarkable amounts of time and other resources to support activities that, for the most part, begin and end near one or another field of play and which do not necessarily extend into other aspects or periods of their lives.

Nevertheless, this restricted dimension of community making has important implications for our understanding of processes of social affiliation and communality in a world of mobile individuals and compartmentalized social lives. It underscores the capacity of mobile strangers to generate spaces and possibilities for fashioning satisfying social connections out of limited, voluntary, but deeply textured and meaningful activities. What it also suggests is that community need not be confined within anthropological thought to being either all-encompassing, essential, abiding and intimate in nature or, alternatively, as merely an outcome of imagination. This chapter analyses a particular sphere of activity where people work hard to construct means of consociation and to make strangers knowable, notwithstanding the limitations of time, space and competing social involvements that confront all suburbanites.

This examination of the organization and maintenance of organized sports for children seeks to identify the salient characteristics of a set of activities, relationships, and attendant meanings that underpin a distinctive form of community. Lacking either ethnic homogeneity or enduring social boundaries to sustain it, the shared consciousness of some degree of commonality as members of one or another local sport group is by no means a given or easily accomplished outcome. Yet under certain conditions, involvement in children's sports yields transitory, but none the less much appreciated experiences of belonging. Social arrangements that encourage and enable suburban residents to connect with one another even briefly in a context that is otherwise characterized by its potential for segmentation, differentiation and isolation are certainly deserving of anthropological attention.[1]

The following section identifies pertinent aspects of the organizational structures and capacities of children's sport activities that equip them to serve as mundane, but effective media for generating relationships and experiences of community.

The organization of children's sports

In Canada community sport clubs and leagues for children and youth operate independently of intra- and extra-mural school sports programmes. Community sports are organized by sport-specific local organizations that are affiliated with provincial, national, and international sport organizations. While extensive use is made by sports clubs of municipal sports facilities (including playing fields, gymnasia, swimming pools, ice rinks, etc.), the administration, officiating, and coaching functions tend to be carried out by unpaid volunteers, most of whom are parents of child athletes. The funding of the operational costs incurred by community sports depends in large part upon membership fees and fund-raising schemes mounted by most local sport organizations.[2]

While the initial financial cost of a child's participation (in terms of registration fees and personal equipment) will vary significantly from one sport to another, there are also more or less substantial and explicit expectations in most community sport organizations about the level of parental participation required. Parental participation minimally involves parents arranging transportation for children to and from weekly practice sessions and competitions, but parents are also encouraged to attend games to 'support' their children and to assist with more or less time-consuming fund-raising activities. A child's ability to participate in community sports without some degree of parental support and participation would be severely constrained. Moreover, parents who have more than one child enrolled in community sports and/or non-sport activities (such as Cubs or music lessons) will normally expect to drive to and from these events on given weeknights as well as to make more substantial investments of time on weekends.

The continued viability of community sports depends upon the support of sufficient numbers of both children and parents. Although children's participation in community sports may be more or less accurately explained by and subsumed under the heading of 'fun', parents' reasons for supporting these activities are more complicated and even somewhat controversial. Interestingly, the stereotypical figure of the parent who is suspected of vicariously pursuing self-aggrandizement through a son's or daughter's athletic success is well known in Canada, not least among parents who themselves make considerable sacrifices to facilitate their children's involvement in sport. Suffice it to say that I have never heard a parent apply this stereotype to him- or herself; it is, rather, an assessment that is directed towards others, and usually to categorical others rather than to known persons.

Why, given these moral suspicions and the burden of demands made of parents for time and money, do so many suburban-dwelling fathers and mothers support their children's participation in community sports even at the most minimal level, let alone at the much higher levels accepted by some couples? The long hours spent on cold and rainy afternoons watching soccer games, the tedious waiting that precedes and follows hockey practices and games scheduled either before or after normal work hours on weekdays and at virtually any time on weekends, and the manner in which parents are effectively forced to interact with other parents with whom they may otherwise have little in common, are all factors that may prompt mothers and fathers to alter, limit or even eliminate their involvement (and likely, thereby, their children's participation) in community sports. Why, then, do so many parents continue to support and to take a greater, smaller, or any part in community sports for children? Concomitantly, what organizational properties allow community sport organizations to sustain themselves despite the shifting currents of internal family dynamics and priorities as well as pervasive patterns of suburban residential mobility?

Sports may be expected to furnish 'fun' for child participants, but parental engagement in these activities constitutes a form of 'hidden work' (Wadel 1979), namely, that of child rearing. Organized sports claim to provide a wholesome and beneficial set of experiences and outcomes for children, and these assertions tend to receive broad, if not unquestioning or uniform, support from Canadian parents. At the very least, organized sports offer a form of adult-controlled activity wherein children are supposed to be protected from the presumed manifold dangers of congregating unsupervised on the 'street'. Sports are also viewed as promoting physical exercise and well-being in addition to diverse social and developmental benefits such as fostering play as team members. Indeed, a recent survey conducted in British Columbia found that:

> parents expect sport participation and sport leaders to be a part of developing their children. Parents expect that playing basketball or field hockey are worthwhile activities in themselves, but only if it provides the value added benefits of building self-esteem and fun.
>
> (SOAR International 1994: 26)

Yet as well as being seen as an effective means for generating self-esteem among children (Dyck 2000b), organized sport is also valued by some parents for the manner in which it introduces their children to competition. From this perspective, sport is interpreted as a field in which children may be appropriately exposed to, and prepared for, the competitive realities of adult life. Although parental disagreement over the relative advantages and disadvantages of stressing competition over participation is frequently encountered, particularly when children are younger, competition remains an essential but controversial feature of children's sport.

Sport is also valued by parents for its intrinsically social nature. Not only does participation in community sport temporarily remove children from watching television or playing computer games, it also brings them into contact with other children. Moreover, it permits sons and daughters to obtain what may be seen as useful experience of dealing with adults in organized activities outside of classroom and familial settings. And not least, children's sports provide a variety of opportunities for parents to meet and spend time with other parents who might be expected to share some common concerns with respect to their mutual involvement in child rearing. Yet the prospect of spending extensive amounts of time with randomly selected aggregations of parents is not necessarily anticipated with enthusiasm by all mothers or fathers. The significance attached to perceived differences in style, taste, and values reflect not only individual preferences, but also the sensitivity and uncertainty of social status and class standing within residentially and socially mobile suburbs. In short, parents prefer to spend time with other parents 'like us' and may seek to avoid or limit the extent to which they must share proximity or be associated with those whom they deem to be 'unlike' themselves. Nevertheless, in order to position themselves to meet desirable persons, parents may well have to tolerate longer or shorter periods at sports events with individuals who are not necessarily companions of choice. The organizational properties of children's sport activities do, however, provide means for balancing these interactional objectives and, in so doing, to nurture relations and experiences of community. This capacity to generate effective, though transitory, links of communal affiliation without resort to or need of long-standing, multiplex or homogeneous relationships is particularly significant in a world of mobile individuals and compartmentalized social lives.

What needs to be underscored is the manner in which parental involvement in community sports for children not only serves to support the individual and shared project of child rearing, but may also facilitate the creation and maintenance of extra-familial relationships and activities for both children and parents, links and events that may evoke a sense of affiliation and community among participants. Honouring the expectations of parent participation set by a given team or club over a season will involve parents in carrying out a variety of support tasks which may range from bringing oranges to soccer matches (for the refreshment of players at half-time), telephoning parents on behalf of the coach to announce changes to the schedule of games and practices, assisting with the hosting of a track meet (Dyck 1995), or even helping to coach a team of beginning soccer players. These tasks can be performed reluctantly or perfunctorily (if one wishes to avoid being asked to assist again) or may be carried out with efficiency and enthusiasm. Even the most tiresome of undertakings – for instance, a car-wash staged by parents to raise funds for a soccer team – can prove to be a surprisingly companionable occasion when, and if, it elicits good humour and a certain degree of playfulness from participating parents.

From these and other incidental contacts may develop not only organizational roles, but also discursive relationships that either remain politely discreet or which may flower into serial conversations which are anticipated and enjoyed by individual parents, who proceed from being recognized faces to named persons who spend much of a season talking to one another. Parents, who comprise much of the audience around a playing field, pool, or ice rink, have ample leeway either to minimize conversation or to talk about the weather, the state of play that they are witnessing, or even of their efforts and concerns as parents. The extent to which individual parents choose to engage in mutual self-presentation and definition is entirely up to them. But the fact that they met and continue to meet one another in the weekly routine of accompanying their children to sport events makes possible the gradual generation of relationships, sport memories, and situationally shared meanings that constitute a form of community that, in turn, recognizes and reaffirms the very existence of any given family. In contrast with traditional and recent anthropological renderings of community, the bonds of affiliation that develop within this setting are neither all encompassing nor simply imagined. Nor are these particular relations of community lightly felt or insignificant to those involved in them.

The capacity of local sport teams and clubs to realize their formal purposes of organizing competitive sport activities for children depends upon an aptitude to sustain the continuing support of enough parents who are seeking roughly similar, but not necessarily identical experiences and outcomes for their children and themselves through participation in sport. The ability of community sports to accommodate these diverse, but none the less related objectives is, I would suggest, attributable to the organizational properties that they share.

First, children's sport possesses a general organizational form that features regularity, predictability, openness, and relative comprehensibility: all factors that enable these organizations to solicit and retain participation by children and parents simply by virtue of their structural durability. Children and parents come and go, but as long as a sufficient number of them take part, at least for the current season in any given community sport, that organization will continue to exist and welcome the next year's group of prospective participants. Second, children's sports are symbolically united and legitimated under a powerful assertion that their programmes are inherently 'good' for children. Since children's sports are categorized not simply as leisure activities, but as an ancillary form of child rearing and development, they come equipped with a definitional plasticity that allows every adult to claim that his or her involvement in these activities is 'for the kids'. This facilitates a symbolic ambiguity that permits virtually every divisive stance and its opposite to be articulated and yet obfuscated in terms of the same overarching credo of self-sacrifice. In any given situation where a proportion of parents may wish to pursue only a moderate to minimal level of involvement in the activities of the club or league, the extent of the actual divergence between their preferences and those of others who wish to take a more active part in setting the agenda for a club or league can be usefully de-emphasized. Activists are, by default, permitted considerable space and opportunity to pursue their own visions of what might be in the 'best interests of the kids'.

Finally, contested or irreconcilable positions can be relieved by dissatisfied parents and their children searching out other options in the broad array of community sports for children. In the meantime, the scale and flexibility of community sports for children enables individual parents and children to search not only for sporting activities, but also for forms of association and experiences of belonging that satisfy their current inclinations. The minimal requirements of sustaining community sport organizations for children serves to bring children and adults in a suburban milieu into contact with one another for ostensibly useful and worthy purposes. What results from these routinized social arrangements may be seen as a contingent, limited, and fleeting sense of community, but it would seem to reflect what is possible in a suburban setting. Nevertheless, the everyday activities comprised by, and associated with, children's sports also offer the circumstances wherein those who are seeking more than this level of practical and superficial involvement and who wish to pursue it with people who seem to be like themselves are enabled to do so. The capacity of community sports as an organizational form to create intense, albeit episodic, opportunities for enhancing experiences of likeness and communality in otherwise heterogeneous suburban social settings is explored in the following section.

'Have you been to Hayward Field?'

During the last two decades of the twentieth century the business of identifying oneself as a Canadian has become a complicated and confusing matter. The constitutional search for national unity in the face of demands for Quebecois sovereignty and the settlement of Aboriginal land claims have occupied much of the federal parliamentary agenda. Moreover, since the late 1980s Canada's entry into the North American Free Trade Agreement has begun to reshape economic practices and social and cultural programmes in controversial and far-reaching ways. Living cheek by jowl with the world's only remaining super power, Canadians have been exhorted by their political leaders to embrace the competitive challenges of continentalism and globalization. Increased levels of immigration have been mooted and implemented as a prerequisite for equipping Canada to face the new millennium, but have left in their wake recurring instances of racist reaction and contentious policies of multiculturalism. In the realm of public rhetoric Canada may be trumpeted as the best of countries in which to live, yet continuing survey research reports that Canadians are seriously divided in their views about the positive and negative effects of current levels of immigration.[3]

At more mundane levels, the negotiation of workable identities and forms of interaction that enable immigrants and native-born Canadians to acknowledge one another's presence and acquire some minimal sense of belonging within the localities they co-inhabit cannot remain merely matters for contemplation. While the stream of pronouncements issued by government agencies and public figures in support of national unity and ethnic tolerance provide little in the way of practical assistance, nevertheless, informal initiatives towards this end are being mounted in neighbourhoods and municipalities as Canadians, native-born and naturalized, set about the quotidian matter of fashioning lives for themselves and their families. Here we shall examine one such instance that illustrates the practices of identity making and affiliation fostered by children's athletics and demonstrates that the construction of certain routinized forms of interaction may offer limited, but effective means for realizing situated senses of belonging and communality. The processes that are of concern here are highlighted and further elaborated when child and parental involvement in these activities takes place both locally and extra-locally.

A sport such as track and field requires particularly substantial levels of parental assistance in order to stage the weekend competitions that local clubs take turns in hosting. Unlike a soccer game that requires only three officials and two coaches, an athletics meet featuring a full range of gender-divided and age-graded disciplinary competitions will seek to enlist as many as 100 adults to organize, officiate, and record the results of competition.[4] Parents can, therefore, anticipate being pressed into service when a club's turn to host a meet comes round again. Fathers and mothers who lack any experience or expertise in athletics are provided on-the-job training, and over time an ambitious track club will endeavour to assemble a set of parent volunteers who have become more or less practised and proficient in satisfying the logistical demands presented in staging an athletics meet.

The particular community athletics club considered here had grown rapidly in a few years, both in terms of the number of its registered athletes and coaches and in its ambitions. As well as attracting and training athletes in the full range of athletics disciplines – sprints, distance running, throws and jumps – it had begun to host not only its own annual club meet, but also larger and organizationally more demanding provincial and national meets. Thus, many parents of the club had, of necessity, assisted in staging a larger or smaller number of time-consuming and physically exhausting track meets, a form of parental self-sacrifice that is typically celebrated as 'doing it for the kids'. Like many community athletics clubs in the Vancouver area, this one had attracted a significant number of immigrant parents and children from many countries, for unlike ice hockey, which is popularly and sometimes aggressively identified as the definitively 'Canadian' game, track and field is a truly global sport.

As the club expanded its membership, its hosting activities, and claims to be one of the leading track and field clubs in the province, other prominent figures in local, provincial, and national track and field circles lost no opportunity to remind the club's leaders that athletics is an international sport and that local glory may represent little more than victories won in a very small pond. Although the club's athletes had enjoyed considerable success against American competitors both in local meets and in visits to meets in nearby Bellingham and Seattle, much stiffer levels of athletic competition and organizational prowess were reported to exist in Eugene, Oregon, the site of Hayward Field, a stadium at the University of Oregon that is specifically designed for, and fully devoted to, track and field. The athletics meet for children and youth held annually at Hayward Field began to loom large in the minds of club officials. Individual coaches and a few of the club's leading athletes began to drive down by car to the annual meet in Eugene and invariably came back with roughly the same message: 'You don't know what track and field is all about until you have been to Eugene.'

My visit to Hayward Field came in the third year that the club chartered a bus to take athletes and parents to Oregon. The group that convened at 3.15 a.m. on that Friday in July comprised eighteen parents (including four coaches), eighteen child and youth athletes (including two who were not accompanied by their parents), two grandparents of athletes, four siblings of athletes, and one friend of an athlete. Two-thirds of the parents had been born outside Canada, and overall the group included adults and the children of immigrants born in Italy, Jamaica, Dominica, Trinidad, Turkey, England, Northern Ireland, the Philippines, Finland, and India.[5] As we stumbled on to the bus for the ten-hour drive to Eugene, one of the coaches who had made the trip in previous years proclaimed, so all could hear, that the first order of business was to have the bus driver remove his necktie for the duration of the trip. 'When this club goes on the road', he explained, 'we always have a good time.'

One might reasonably harbour certain misgivings about the prospects of a 'good time' emanating from two ten-hour bus rides and two nights and three days spent at close quarters in fast-food restaurants, motel hallways, and the hard wooden seats of Hayward Field in the company of more than forty adults and children. Indeed, while most of the departing passengers knew each other at least by sight and some by name, there was considerable variation in the extent to which the parents, at least, had worked with one another at club meets or interacted informally prior to this trip. None the less, the trip did turn out to be a remarkably enjoyable and memorable experience.

What parents of athletes have in common is that they are parents who share a common concern with child rearing and also at least some minimal experience with the routines of club athletic involvement which engage their children and them. Being a parent who is situationally recognized as being involved in children's athletics makes one eligible to claim or to be accorded a formal or categorical identity of 'track parent'. Yet, beyond this relatively impersonal form of identification lies the possibility of what Sansom identifies as consociate identity which is constructed 'with reference to a person's history of co-participation with others in happenings' (1980: 139). Consociate relationships emerge when individuals become capable of putting names to known faces and telling stories about mutually shared experiences in the world of track and field (Dyck 1995). This trip to Hayward Field, like any weekend spent at a track meet, yielded a set of more or less amusing and recountable 'happenings' that were shared and corroborated in subsequent encounters, whether at the local track or in a chance encounter between parents at a neighbourhood supermarket.

Nevertheless, this visit to Hayward Field had outcomes beyond those triggered by participation in local track meets, and it is to these that I turn in the remainder of this chapter. The message that 'you don't know what track and field is all about until you have been to Eugene' is one that is, to put it mildly, nurtured by Oregonian track officials. Their track meet, entitled the 'Track City Classic' was subsidized in part by the sale of T-shirts emblazoned with the words, 'I was at the Classic (ask me about it)'. The opening ceremonies of the meet featured a parade of athletes marching by club around the stadium and a speech by the athletics director of the University of Oregon. Noting that this parade replicates the ceremonial forms of the Olympic Games, the athletics director went on to pay homage to Hayward Field, his university's facility, a site which he claimed was often referred to as the 'Carnegie Hall' of track and field. Citing the many times that the Olympic selection trials for the United States track and field team have been staged in this stadium, he characterized Hayward Field as a place that attracts and encourages the best in athletic performance. He finished by observing that this particular meet had brought together the future hopes for American track and field. While both the American and Canadian national anthems were played at the end of the march past, never once did the speaker note the presence of Canadian athletes at the meet. This was commented upon by several of the club parents with whom I sat in the stands. Concerning the parade of athletes, a ceremonial form included in provincial or national, but never in club meets staged in British Columbia, one of our number simply observed that 'Americans love to march in parades'.

Child and youth athletes from the club scored quite respectable performances at the meet, particularly in field events and middle- and long-distance races. Even in the sprint events, which were dominated by athletes from several California clubs, two of our sprinters made the finals of their respective events, but did not 'medal'. This prompted one of the California sprint coaches to inquire concerning the qualifying standards set by our club for membership. He was surprised to learn that any child could join the club, no matter the level of his or her athletic performance. In turn, the parents with whom he spoke were amazed to learn of the levels of corporate sponsorship enjoyed by his and other American track clubs. In later discussions, club parents contrasted the implicitly 'professional' approach of the American clubs, with an emphasis upon producing top results, with their own parent-funded and -coached club under the familiar self-praising theme that 'we are only here for the kids'. One of the club mothers directed our attention to the 'hard eyes' of the American athletes: 'tough little nuts who have seen a lot of competition'. In comparison, she claimed, 'our kids seem quite innocent'.

While those club parents who were visiting Hayward Field for the first time marvelled at the amount and technological sophistication of the track equipment and timing devices furnished by meet officials, they were forewarned by others to keep an eye out for officiating errors of the sort that frequently occur at track meets. In fact, notwithstanding the readily apparent confidence displayed by meet officials, a number of such errors were detected, and several of these were formally and successfully appealed by club coaches and parents on behalf of their children.[6]

These and other shortcomings of the meet were carefully noted and discussed at length by members of the group, who concluded that 'We put on a track meet just about as well as they do at Hayward Field.' Although suitably impressed with the specialized facilities and levels of competition to be found in Eugene, the coaches and parents of the club came away from Eugene with renewed appreciation of their own individual and collective level of expertise in hosting and appreciating track and field. Although the terms selected to identify the group being recognized were 'us' and 'our club' rather than 'Canadian', the cumulative contrast drawn between the 'Americans' and 'us' signalled a collectively experienced self-identification by those who got back on the bus for the long trip back to British Columbia. When the journey ended on Monday at 3.00 a.m. in the shopping centre parking lot, more than a few parents called out 'goodnight, everyone' as they headed into the darkness to find their parked cars. No longer persons who knew one another only by sight, they had travelled together to Hayward Field, purchased T-shirts which attested to their presence at the 'Classic', and would talk about it among themselves and with others for the remainder of that summer and in track seasons to come.

Above and beyond what community sport clubs may provide child and youth athletes in the way of physical exercise, competitive opportunities, sociability, and, not least, fun, they also afford parents with routinized and relatively predictable institutional forms with which to supplement the tasks of child rearing. Parental involvement in a sport such as athletics may be kept at a relatively superficial level or, depending upon one's preferences and resources of time and money, may be entered into more fully. Engagement of this sort readily generates the types of happenings essential to the creation of consociate identities and putative declarations of affiliation and community. Limited though even these forms of parental interaction may be, they do offer the prospect of some sense of communality and belonging in otherwise largely anonymous urban and suburban settings. But when children's sport activities begin to be pursued beyond the local level, the logistical and social arrangements that such undertakings necessitate are likely to be compounded with new sets of encountered cultural definitions and distinctions out of which more elaborated senses of similarity and community – if not national unity – may be fashioned. As the case presented here demonstrates, when the participants in such ventures come from widely diverging backgrounds, experiences of shared travel have the capacity to furnish new, albeit highly situated, identities which can be discovered and enjoyed on the road and then taken 'home'.

Mundane stuff, no doubt, but as one of the Jamaican-born fathers in the club expressed it to me one evening on the balcony of our motel in Eugene, 'They say that there is no utopia, but, hey, I'm here with my family, having a good time. What else is there?'

For anthropologists interested in the constitution and dynamics of community, there is something more to note. By travelling to places like Hayward Field and braving the risk of discovering and revealing themselves to be, perhaps, very small frogs in an infinitely larger pond, the members of an expedition such as this one acknowledge and embrace the thoroughly global nature of activities such as track and field. In doing so, their shared travel and participation become transformative experiences. They, too, are now able to declare (as they most certainly have done) that 'you don't know what track and field is all about until you have been to Eugene', a claim that entitles its speaker to be identified – at least in the western part of North America – as someone who 'really knows track and field'. As yet, relatively few parent participants in track and field are positioned to make such a claim.

Paradoxically, however, the more lasting effects of moving beyond the local is the creation of a set of shared, but highly specific experiences, relationships, and identities that can be taken back to particular localities and interactional settings and employed and enjoyed in quite specialized roles with limited numbers of people. Thus, the everyday activities and interactions of otherwise separate and distinct lives and identities are overlaid with partial, but none the less vital interests, relationships, memories, sentiments, and identities that are shared with at least a few of one's neighbours. In these circumstances, where 'you' and 'I' come from becomes less significant than where 'we' have been and may go next.

Conclusions

This examination of the use of organized sport for children and youth as a malleable medium for constructing varied notions and relations of community in a suburban locale is offered not as a general recipe for contemporary community. It does, however, speak to the determination of people to search for, and sometimes to realize, delimited but satisfying experiences of social connection and belonging even in suburban settings. Significantly, the forms of communality generated through sport participation in this reputedly inauspicious setting are neither merely imagined nor constricted within the tightly encapsulated roles associated with older conventional renderings of community. Instead, the established routines of sport clubs and leagues for children and youth in suburban British Columbia provide durable organizational forms and relationships capable of accommodating considerable social flexibility for individual participants. The organizational structures of children's sport are annually renewed by the return of some child and youth athletes and their parents and the arrival of others who are new to a given club, league or sport. The operational requirements of most sport organizations are sufficiently transparent and manageable to survive turnover in personnel year by year.

Sport organizations typically pre-exist and survive any given set of individual athletes and parents who, for one or more seasons, play more or less prominent parts in the activities of teams and clubs. Adult participants enjoy some leeway in determining the nature and extent of their involvement in children's sport, notwithstanding the periodic efforts of some club and team officials to enforce prescribed standards of parental participation. Parents who are determined to limit the demands made upon their own time, energies, and finances by children's sport attempt to develop more suitable versions of parent participation that may involve simply providing transportation to and from practices and games and seldom leaving their cars to venture towards playing fields, rinks or swimming pools. A few parents even leave their children to arrange their own rides to sport activities with either coaches or other parents until polite tolerance for continued failure to reciprocate sooner or later puts an end to this and, possibly, to the child's ability to partake of the sport. At the other end of the spectrum are parents who attend virtually every game and practice and invariably make themselves available to assist coaches and to converse with other parents at sports events. Between these two extremes parents can exercise considerable latitude in determining styles and levels of participation suited to their circumstances and inclinations. And while most parents appreciate the merits of remaining judiciously 'friendly', those who wish to venture beyond this amiable, but circumspect stance to seek increasing familiarity with other parents can do so without these initiatives becoming particularly obvious.

In moving from impersonality to engagement, sport parents shift from being merely contemporaries to becoming consociates. These consociate relationships are enacted primarily within the context of sporting events including training sessions, games, tournaments, fund-raising activities, award banquets, and travel to places such as Hayward Field. Friendships formed in these settings sometimes lead to friendships that operate beyond this sphere, but this outcome is not necessary in order for parents involved in children's sport to develop a much-appreciated sense of affiliation with other parents. The capacity of children's sports to generate satisfying experiences of community depends upon the balancing of durable organizational forms with social flexibility that enables and encourages parents to fashion varied, situationally limited yet transitory relationships that, none the less, afford them satisfying experiences of belonging and communality.

The ethnographic account and analysis presented in this chapter speaks directly to our understanding of processes of affiliation and community making in a world otherwise characterized by social mobility and compartmentalization that serve to isolate people. In particular, it underlines an inconspicuous, but effective means by which residents of Canadian suburbs are enabled to access and exploit opportunities for pursuing meaningful and highly textured social connections within an otherwise inauspicious and impersonal social setting. In conclusion, anthropologists would be well advised not only to look beyond categorical definitions of community that remain socially inchoate, but also to lighten the notional burden and requisite components placed on this concept. As this chapter demonstrates, the achievement of some simple, but eminently satisfying forms of social connection and belonging do not require that relations of communality become all-encompassing and directive in nature. Individuality and choice need not be compromised in order to establish and enjoy community.

Notes

1 This position has been lucidly presented by Vered Amit both in her earlier publications (Amit-Talai 1994a, 1994b) and in our recent discussions of this issue. I also wish to express my appreciation for her critical, but most helpful comments on earlier drafts of this chapter while at the same time absolving her of responsibility for the final form of this chapter.

2 A broad range of sports are made available by local organizations in British Columbia, including athletics, baseball, bowling, figure skating, (Canadian) football, gymnastics, ice hockey, ringette, speed skating, lacrosse, martial arts, soccer, softball, speed and synchronized swimming, water polo, and tennis. Participation of children by age and gender varies from sport to sport, but there are many local sport organizations catering to boys and girls between the ages of approximately 5 and 17 years. Between the ages of 5 and 10 years, as many as 50 per cent of the children in one suburban area participated for longer or shorter periods in one or more community sport organizations (Dyck and Wildi 1993).

3 Expressed concern about the stresses placed upon the economy and social infrastructure by high levels of immigration is particularly evident in the metropolitan centres of Toronto, Montreal, and, most of all, Vancouver, which are the preferred settlement locations for 60 per cent of immigrants. See Vancouver *Sun*, 12 October 1999, 'Vancouver residents most negative towards immigrants: Prejudice increases in direct parallel to the numbers of immigrants.'

4 Ideally, this number should not include the host club's volunteer coaches, who ought to be fully occupied with assisting the club's own child and youth athletes.

5 Other members of the club from West Africa and the United States had opted to drive themselves to and from the meet.

6 For instance, a video-taped recording (shot from the stands by one of the fathers in the club) of the finish of one race demonstrated that a club athlete had finished fifth rather than seventh in the 100 metre final for her age-category. While the faulty placing of this athlete was not significant for the outcome of the meet, the final time awarded to this athlete was her personal best in this event for the season.

References

Amit-Talai, Vered (1994a) 'Connections: The Ethnographic Challenge', in V. Amit-Talai and H. Lustiger-Thaler (eds) *Urban Lives: Fragmentation and Resistance*, Toronto: McClelland and Stewart, pp. 121–8.

Amit-Talai, Vered (1994b) 'Urban Pathways: The Logistics of Youth Peer Relations', in V. Amit-Talai and H. Lustiger-Thaler (eds) *Urban Lives: Fragmentation and Resistance*, Toronto: McClelland and Stewart, pp. 183–205.

Bellah, R. N, R. Madsen, W. M. Sullivan, A. Swidler, and S. M. Tipton (1985) *Habits of the Heart: Individualism and Commitment in American Life*, Berkeley: University of California Press.

Cohen, Anthony P. (1985) *The Symbolic Construction of Community*, London: Tavistock, and Ellis Horwood Ltd.

——(1987) *Whalsay: Symbol, Segment and Boundary in a Shetland Island Community*, Manchester: Manchester University Press.

Dyck, Noel (1995) 'Parents, Consociates and the Social Construction of Children's Athletics', *Anthropological Forum*, 7, 2: 215–29.

——(2000a) 'Home Field Advantage? Exploring the Social Construction of Children's Sports', in Vered Amit (ed.) *Constructing the 'Field': Ethnographic Fieldwork at the Turn of the Century*, London and New York: Routledge pp. 32–53.

——(2000b) 'Parents, Kids and Coaches: Constructing Sport and Childhood in Canada', in Noel Dyck (ed.) *Games, Sports and Cultures*, Oxford and New York: Berg Publishers.

Dyck, Noel and Grant Wildi (1993) *Creating Community Sport for Kids: A Survey of Community Sport Clubs and Associations for Children and Youth in Coquitlam, Port Coquitlam, and Port Moody British Columbia, During the 1992–3 Season*, Burnaby, British Columbia: Department of Sociology and Anthropology, Simon Fraser University.

Fine, Gary Alan and Jay Mechling (1991) 'Minor Difficulties: Changing Children in the Late Twentieth Century', in Alan Wolfe (ed.) *America at Century's End*, Berkeley, Los Angeles and London: University of California Press, pp. 58–78.

Fishman, Robert (1987) *Bourgeois Utopia: The Rise and Fall of Suburbia*, New York: Basic Books.

Gusfield, Joseph R. (1975) *Community: A Critical Response*, Oxford: Basil Blackwell.

Rapport, Nigel (1996) 'Community', in Alan Barnard and Jonathen Spencer (eds) *Encyclopedia of Social and Cultural Anthropology*, London and New York: Routledge, pp. 114–17.

Richards, Lyn (1990) *Nobody's Home: Dreams and Realities in a New Suburb*, Melbourne: Oxford University Press.

Sansom, Basil (1980) *The Camp at Wallaby Cross: Aboriginal Fringe Dwellers in Darwin*, Canberra: Australian Institute of Aboriginal Studies.

SOAR International (1994) *Sport Parent Survey,* Victoria: prepared for the British Columbia Ministry of Government Services, Sports and Commonwealth Games Division.

Wadel, Cato (1979) 'The Hidden Work of Everyday Life', in Sandra Wallman (ed.) *Social Anthropology of Work,* London: Academic Press, pp. 365–84.

Chapter 7

The ethnographic field revisited

Towards a study of common and not so common fields of belonging

Karen Fog Olwig

The nature of the link between community, place and culture has been questioned from different vantage points in anthropology.[1] Students of globalization and migration have noted that the interconnected and mobile lives that people lead today cannot be captured through fieldwork in local sites that are expected to correspond with cultural wholes. Such lives call, rather, for studies of the complex, non-local socio-cultural contexts that characterize modern human existence. Anthropologists who have examined how culture is perceived and practised at an individual level, however, have argued that there never was a close fit between local communities and shared culture. This becomes clear once one abandons the study of generalized cultural wholes and focuses, instead, upon individual lives. Communities or shared fields of belonging are cultural constructions, and the various ways in which they are imagined and sustained by individuals and collectivities, they argue, should be the object of anthropological study. In this chapter I shall examine the kinds of communities and fields of belonging that emerge in the life stories of two men of Caribbean background living in England as they define a place for themselves in the modern world of mobility and interconnectedness. The analysis is based on life story interviews carried out with members of the global family networks of which these men are part. The life stories related by the two persons examined here suggest that a variety of social, economic and cultural factors, grounded in local as well as in global relationships, come into play in the construction and sustaining of communities. I therefore conclude that while it is important for anthropologists to explore the constructed and diffuse nature of many communities today, it is equally, if not more important, to ground studies of such communities in the concrete fields of social relations and cultural values within which they are imagined and realized. I end the chapter by calling into question the usefulness of the notion of diasporic

community, which is being used today in many works on transnationalism and globalization. I argue that this term evokes generalized ideas of
communities of belonging rooted in distant homelands, often espoused
by third world intellectuals, that may prove to be too simplified when
examined against the multifaceted life experiences of those supposed to
belong to these communities.

The ethnography of communities

Anthropologists have usually regarded their sites of field research as constituting some sort of community in the form of a group of people who
believe that they share certain social ties and cultural values which are of
importance to their sense of well-being. In the last few decades, however,
there has been increasing uncertainty as to what the nature of such communities might be at a time when population movements and
globalization seem to wreak havoc with any kind of close-knit, stable and
localized community. A useful new approach can be found in the suggestion that neither past nor present communities should necessarily be
regarded as concrete, physical entities situated in particular places, but
rather as cultural constructions that provide important symbolic as well
as practical frameworks of life.

Two, closely related, notions of community as a cultural construction
have emerged in recent years. These notions have been applied to different ethnographic situations and entail different methodological
approaches. The first casts communities as entities of 'belonging' and has
emerged in studies of modern complex societies, most notably rural
areas in Great Britain. The other line of research views community as a
more imagined entity rooted in 'sentiment'. The first approach has
involved in-depth fieldwork-based ethnographic research of rural villages as sites where various forms of socio-economic interests and cultural
identification are played out and contested among people interacting in
close, face-to-face relationships (A. P. Cohen 1982; Strathern 1982;
Rapport 1993; for a Scandinavian example see Ekman 1991). In recent
studies there has been an interest in examining the individuality of particular members of communities as they work out their understanding of
social life and personalize their identities, including national identities
(A. P. Cohen 1996; Rapport 1997). This first approach thus exhibits a
movement away from regarding community as a collective unit encompassing individuals, towards a focusing on the ways in which community
is constructed through the negotiation of meaning among interacting
persons.

The second notion of community has been advanced to shed light on the development of more extensive constructs that cannot be experienced directly through personal inter-relationships, but more indirectly through the generating of feelings believed to be shared by a larger collectivity. This approach developed first in studies of the emergence of modern nations termed 'imagined communities' by Benedict Anderson (1983). This concept has been further elaborated by Arjun Appadurai (1996) in his research on the modern, interconnected world of migration and mass media, where 'individual attachments, interests, and aspirations increasingly crosscut those of the nation-state' (Appadurai 1996: 10). In this world, according to Appadurai, communities of primary importance become those of 'sentiment' which emerge as groups of people begin 'to imagine and feel things together' (ibid.: 8). Such communities presumably exist at many different levels of life, but they are particularly apparent in 'the widespread appearance of various kinds of diasporic public spheres', expressed through the arts or transnational ethnic politics, and they constitute, for Appadurai 'one special diacritic of the global modern' (ibid.: 11). Such spheres are, according to Appadurai, 'frequently tied up with students and other intellectuals engaging in long-distance nationalism' (ibid.: 22). This approach therefore, primarily, lets relatively few, well-articulated individuals speak for these communities. The same trend is apparent in the work on transnationalism (which for Appadurai is closely related to these public spheres). The notion of transnationalism draws attention to the development of ethnic, or national, fields of social, economic, political ties and cultural values transcending political borders in connection with migration from one nation state to another. While some authors (Schiller et al. 1992; Bash et al. 1994) have emphasized that transnational communities are grounded in people's every-day lives, they have tended to focus on communities based on ethnic politics. Such communities are often organized by educated migrants of middle-class background. By evoking the notion of transnational communities, these political actors are able to exploit their dual position as a potentially powerful social, economic and political force in their country of origin, and as a growing minority in their country of residence subject to, but also able to take advantage of, ethnic politics in this country (Kearney 1995; Mahler 1998).[2] Research which takes its point of departure in the 'public diasporic sphere' therefore has tended to examine public forms of representation of the more diffuse, global communities of sentiment.

While the two notions of community which emerge from these recent studies may seem rather similar in that they both see community as a cultural construction with a strong symbolic dimension, they lead to quite different ethnographic approaches. Communities of 'belonging', as studied in rural Western societies, are viewed as contested fields of interaction and negotiation based in concrete fields of face-to-face social relationships and reflecting a great deal of individuality and active participation on the part of their members. Communities of 'sentiment' have been salient in research on migrant urban populations originating primarily in the third world. These communities are examined in terms of artistic expressions and/or organized national/ethnic politics that are supposed to reflect the concerns of diffuse communities rooted in distant homelands. We are therefore in the rather paradoxical situation that the complexity of life in the modern world of globalization and population mobility now tends to be examined primarily in terms of formalized, collective representations of localized groups of diasporic intellectuals and transnational ethnic politicians, while the simpler forms of existence in local rural communities are treated in terms of increasingly complex patterns of individual contestation embedded in intricate and dynamic webs of close and personal inter-relationships. This role reversal probably reflects a felt need to simplify the complex modern world in terms of somewhat organized and manageable fieldsites, and to explore the possible complexities of the seemingly simple fieldsites in the orderly, traditional world of rural communities (see also Olwig 1997). It is also indicative of the ways in which anthropologists have conceptualized local and global communities. Anthropologists have thus regarded local communities as being grounded in consciously localized face-to-face relations, whereas they have seen global communities as dispersed fields of relations that can be imagined as entities of identification, but not experienced through direct interpersonal relations pertaining to everyday life. This analysis shows, however, that the experience of community that emerges when focusing on particular individuals is based on close, personal inter-relationships of local as well as global dimensions, and that this intimate sphere of experience informs the ways in which more generalized forms of ethnic, or diasporic, identification are envisioned. This chapter therefore argues that it is important to examine concrete instances of community formation as experienced by particular individuals, rather than take a point of departure in presumed categories of ethnic, diasporic or transnational communities.

In a critique of the tendency to examine identities in terms of categorical entities Somers (1994) has proposed that a narrative approach allows for an examination of how individuals construct identities in concrete temporal, spatial and relational contexts, both as specific historical persons and as members of wider societal orders. She thus views life as basically 'storied' in the sense that it is through the construction and relating of narratives that persons create some sort of order and meaning in their lives, both as individual persons with specific life trajectories of their own and as social persons who belong to particular communities of relations. Narratives therefore allow for the elucidation of the sort of communities of belonging with which persons identify in different contexts of life. I would suggest that a narrative approach is particularly useful when examining communities, and the forms of identity formation, that are sustained by persons who are not necessarily interacting within the same physical space, but who may, nevertheless, maintain a strong feeling of relatedness through time by telling stories to and/or about each other. This is the case when studying people who have lived in quite different places at different stages of their lives because of migratory moves.

Since 1996 I have carried out life story interviews in three family networks of Caribbean background who have been subject to a great deal of migration, with the consequence that members now live in North America and Europe as well as the Caribbean.[3] As a form of narrative, a life story entails an accounting of an individual's movements through time in such a way that it portrays a sense of coherence reflective of the narrator's sense of self (Peacock and Holland 1993; Gullestad 1994; Ochs and Capps 1996). These narratives are created out of the welter of occurrences and relationships which characterizes most lives; but they also comply with certain cultural values, because they need to follow certain established norms concerning what kind of a life is credible and socially acceptable. By asking people to relate their life stories, we may therefore obtain data on the socio-cultural order which these people establish in their life stories and their own particular understanding of themselves in this order. We may, in other words, ascertain the kind of communities of belonging and sentiment within which they inscribe themselves from their particular social, economic, geographic and personal vantage point. Life stories elicited in global fields of family relations can shed light upon one another, both in terms of the information provided, and in terms of the significance that the wider, non-local community of interpersonal family relations may have had for the narrators.

The three family networks that I have interviewed are the bilateral descendants of three couples born during the period from the late nineteenth to the early twentieth century on the West Indian islands of Jamaica, Dominica and Nevis. These couples are all deceased now, except for one person, the 'matriarch' of the Jamaican family who was born in

1900. The families were chosen so that different islands and somewhat different class and racial backgrounds would be represented. The Jamaican family has a middle-class background in business, the Dominican family a lower middle-class background in school teaching and small farming, and the Nevisian family a lower-class background in small farming and plantation work. They are all racially mixed, the Dominican family generally being the lightest (with some members passing as white outside the Caribbean) and the Nevisian family the darkest. Most persons interviewed (a total of approximately 150 people) readily identify themselves as descendants of the ancestral couple and are able to talk about other descendants. Few family members have extensive knowledge of all the descendants, however, and there is great variation in the significance which individuals attribute to family in general, and specific relatives in particular. This would be expected when working with a group who, though descending from a pair of ancestors, basically function within bilateral family networks. This variation also reflected the fact that the family networks comprised up to four generations of people who were living in different parts of the world under a great variety of social and economic conditions. The family networks therefore constituted rather loose fields of partially shared social ties and cultural values.

Many of the individuals interviewed in this research can be described loosely as part of the Caribbean 'diaspora' to the extent that they live outside their, or their parents', place of birth in the Caribbean. I, however, have not sought to classify them, beforehand, as primarily 'Caribbean', 'diasporic' or as 'migrants', nor have I attempted to frame them within a community of belonging derived from their Caribbean origin. Within the context of family relatedness, I have rather allowed more specific communities of identification to emerge through the life stories which individual family members have related to me. I have done so in order to explore the variety and similarities in the contexts of life which the members constructed as relevant frameworks within which to present and explicate their life trajectories.

I shall here discuss two persons' life stories in terms of the communities of belonging and sentiment, which emerged from their narratives. These life stories are presented on the basis of fieldwork, which I carried out in England in the summer of 1996 at an early stage of the project. They are narrated by two men, part of the family networks of respectively Nevisian and Jamaican origin. Their narratives show that the sort of communities that they imagine, and practice, through their storied lives are influenced by a range of variables that defy easy classification in terms of ethnic, migrant or diasporic labels.

Two narratives

I A narrative of home

I had known Edwin[4] and his relatives for many years when I asked him to tell me his life story. I had first met his sister and several of her relatives in 1974–5, when I did fieldwork in the American Virgin Islands where they were living. In the late 1970s, when I began to do fieldwork on Nevis, I became acquainted with several other sisters and nephews and nieces. When I finally looked up Edwin in Leeds in 1982, I was welcomed as a long-time acquaintance of the family. I remained in contact with Edwin and his family during several periods of fieldwork in Leeds in the late 1980s, and later on I followed their whereabouts through other family members whom I saw in Nevis or the Virgin Islands. Through my long relationship with this family I had therefore had a first-hand experience of family life on a world-wide scale, and when I began a research project on global family networks, it was natural to ask Edwin and his extensive family to participate in this project.

In June 1996 I travelled again to Edwin's family, who had then moved to a somewhat more up-scale neighbourhood just outside Chapel Town, in order to do life story interviews with them. Edwin and his wife Syvilla were busy preparing for their approaching trip to Nevis to participate in Edwin's brother's wedding a few weeks later, where Edwin would be best man. Syvilla, in particular, had spent a great deal of time at the market in Leeds looking for bargains. She needed to bring a large number of gifts, and she had to be sure to wear the variety of clothes that would be suitable to a visitor coming home from abroad. Indeed, by the time I arrived Syvilla had accumulated such a huge pile of items that she felt the need to do a trial packing to ensure that it would be possible to carry everything along.

During this period leading up to the trip to Nevis, where almost the entire family would be together again for the first time since Edwin's mother's funeral a couple of years earlier, Edwin talked a great deal about 'home'. It was clear, however, that Edwin was using the notion of 'home' in at least two different ways. 'Home' meant both a dwelling and a more general community of belonging, but, for Edwin, the two were closely inter-related, so that ideally they were located in the same place. Several important shifts in his perception of home had occurred through time, however, and an important driving force in Edwin's life had been the attempt to reconcile his ideal of home as a place of both independent domestic life, and of belonging in a wider community. Edwin began his life story in this way:

I was born in the West Indies, left when I was 19 years old. As a young lad, after I had left school, I went to learn with a joiner, but I found that the bosses *back home* would not pay any money, because they were teaching you a trade. So I found it hard to survive. I worked all day, still I had to get dinner money from my mother. She had a lot of children to support, and it was hard for her to have me be dependent on her. So I had to find something. I went fishing, because this was the best-paid job in the islands, and I did this until I was ready to come to this country.

A lot of people were leaving for different parts of the world: America, the Virgin Islands and this country. Syvilla's parents sent her here, and I decided to come along, so we came here together on the same boat. We went to Oxford, but there were few Black people in Oxford, so I didn't feel *at home*. I wrote to my uncle and he told me that most of my school mates were here, so one Sunday morning I packed up and went here. A week later Syvilla followed me. We started to look for a place to live. We had one child, Patrick, and we left him behind with his grandparents. We couldn't bring him, we were young, and we didn't know the situation here. We sent for him later and he came along.

Life was hard, there were no rooms to rent, and we had to struggle from place to place. The facilities were bad, the people were arrogant, and we had to move on. We were like fugitives, moving from one place to another. Finally, we got a corporation flat. There were fewer looking for corporation flats at that time, so it was easier to get one, so we were able to get one. The flat was not A1, it was in bad condition, but we had to put up with it. We left this apartment for a corporation house. It was more beneficial with both upstairs and downstairs (the flat only had upstairs). If there are more than one family in a house, nobody cleans the passage, thinking that the others must do this. And you want this tidy. We lived in the house for quite a few years.

In 1975 I went to Nevis. Most West Indians came here expecting to go back in six months, having earned enough money to return. When I went back in 1975 I felt that there was nothing for the kids there. There were better opportunities for education in England than *back home*. I realized that if I went *back home* it would only be Syvilla and I, and we would go when we had retired. So I decided to get my *own home*. You couldn't bring up kids in a corporation house. And if you keep paying rent for a corporation house, you will leave empty-handed when you want to go back to Nevis. I purchased the first house in 1976. It was in bad condition, so I got it cheap. I put a lot of hard work and money into it. When the house was in shape and the children had grown up, they didn't want to stay in the area. It is a self-inflicted problem for the Black people living there. The area got a bad name, and the children didn't want to stay there. So we sold and moved out. We decided to buy this house [emphasis added].

In this introduction to his life story, Edwin operates with three notions of home: *back home*, referring to the island of Nevis where he was born and spent the early part of his life; *at home*, designating a feeling of being part of a local milieu; and *own home*, meaning a physical dwelling owned by Edwin. Briefly summarized, Edwin had to leave *back home*, because he earned below subsistence wages there, so that he had to remain dependent upon his mother, and was not able to get his *own home*. When he left for England, he decide to move to Leeds, where he felt *at home* living in the vicinity of school mates and an uncle from *back home*. He had a major struggle, because he did not have his *own home*, not just because he could not afford one, but also because he expected his stay in England to be brief and to return to Nevis and build a home there. A visit to Nevis convinced him that his children would not like to live there, and so he decided to settle in Leeds and purchased his *own home* in the West Indian community in Chapel Town. When his children became older and refused to remain in Chapel Town, which had acquired a bad reputation, he moved to a new home just outside Chapel Town.

In the late 1980s, after almost 30 years' struggle in England, Edwin seemed to have, finally, relocated himself and created a new home and community of belonging in England. He had a house of his own, which reflected positively upon his achievements in England. Furthermore, this house, being just outside Chapel Town, accommodated both the wishes of his now grown children to avoid the social problems associated with that area and Edwin's desire to socialize with friends in the West Indian community in Chapel Town. This socializing had, for many years, been based in the West Indian Centre, and had involved participation in domino games as well as more organized activities such as fund-raising dinner dances and picnics for senior citizens from the West Indies. Some of these events were also of a more regional nature, such as the cultural festivals, or carnivals, which took place in different cities during the summer months, or the funerals of fellow islanders living in northern or central England. During my stay with Edwin, for example, we went by hired bus to Birmingham to attend a funeral of a Nevisian who was a cousin of one of Edwin's best friends in Leeds. Edwin can thus be described as being part of a strong West Indian community rooted in Chapel Town, the local area where most members of this community congregated and interacted, as well as in the more distant, native island of Nevis from whence his closest friends in the West Indian community derived. Like Edwin, most of these friends had left family on Nevis, most notably parents and siblings, and kept in close contact with them through regular remittances and periodic visits.

Edwin, and his fellow Nevisians would, one might think, feel *at home*, *back home* on Nevis as well as in England, where they had acquired their *own home* and recreated a local West Indian community. This, unfortunately, is not the happy conclusion to which Edwin comes in his life story. Much of his life narrative details his bitterness over the way he has been treated at his place of employment in Great Britain:

> I have suffered a lot here. People of different race will always think they are better than you. But I have my own ideas that I want to use for my own benefit. When I am back here [after the holiday on Nevis] I will have to think about what to do with the rest of my life until I retire. I do not feel I deserve this pushing after 30 years of dedicated work and loyal support at my work place. I should be treated better. They know why they treat me like this, I know why they do it – it is because I am Black. But I don't like to say this when it may be printed in a book.

This kind of treatment made Edwin wish to leave the country and move back to Nevis as soon as retirement would allow him to do so. This desire was, furthermore, spurred by the fact that a number of his good mates had already left and built retirement homes on Nevis. It was apparent to Edwin, however, that moving back to Nevis did not just entail reactivating the home on his natal island, which he had long been celebrating with friends in Chapel Town and maintained through close family ties. Edwin's feeling of having a *home* on Nevis was less firm after his long absence in England:

> No matter where I go Nevis is *home*. I have lived more years here (from the age of 19 to 54, which is what I am now), but I still feel Nevis is where I want to go back to when I retire. I feel more secure there. The place is poor, and there are no facilities, but it is nice. It

may not be as pretty as some of the neighbouring islands, but any place where you can go to sleep at night without locking your door is nice.

Some of the people in Nevis are critical of people who have been away, especially if they are from England. People from America and the Virgin Islands are better treated, they don't get so many remarks. I think it has to do with the way the British government has treated South Africa and other places like that. I can understand the dissatisfaction with that, but why do they have to take it out on us?

The people there do it out of ignorance. I find it hard to take, so I keep a low profile. I try not to talk about politics, when I am in Nevis. Nevis politics can get you into a lot of trouble, so I try not to get involved in it. But anybody can feel free and happy to go to Nevis. You never have to worry about people sneaking up behind you, doing something to you. Nevis is the nicest place on earth [emphasis added].

Edwin's relationship to his family was not without its problems either after the death of both parents a few years previously. The heirs, Edwin and his siblings, found it difficult to agree on how to divide the estate left after the death of the parents, and it was uncertain whether he would be able to acquire a plot on which to build a house. This was a blow to Edwin, because it would be inconceivable for him to return to Nevis without building a good house that could reflect well upon his status as a returnee who had done well abroad:

I now know what I would like my house to be like, and I think that I can build something that I can enjoy. This is what I have worked hard for. I would like people to come and admire my house, and I would like to sit on the veranda and be comfortable, having a drink. I would like a nice bungalow, not all under one roof, but maybe a drop roof. I want three bedrooms, spacious, a dining room, which opens into a sitting room. I want a drive in and a big lawn and a flower garden. The house that I have now is rubbish compared to what I would like to have *at home* [emphasis added].

When I visited Edwin he was quite preoccupied with how he was going to acquire this dream house, where he might live comfortably as a respected member of the local community. When he had done so, he could move away from England, and, finally, make Nevis his permanent home.

2 A narrative of mixing

I knew very little of Henry, and his relatives, when he came to pick me up outside the Sheldonian Theatre in Oxford, an afternoon in July 1996, to drive me to his home in a small rural village nearby. I had just started interviews with this family of Jamaican origin a few days earlier, when I met Henry's sister in London and a brother who happened to be visiting from New Jersey. A fellow migration scholar, who had been a friend of the family for a number of years, had recommended this family as an interesting group of people to work with because it was of middle-class background and had experienced a fair amount of geographic mobility. While most members of Edwin's family were located in Nevis and the two original migration destinations (Great Britain and the American and British Virgin Islands), very few members of the Jamaican family could be found in Jamaica or in the early migration destinations in North America and Great Britain. The family members, instead, were scattered in six different American states, three Canadian provinces, England as well as the West Indian islands of Dominica and, of course, Jamaica. Henry lived in a tiny rural village in the vicinity of Oxford.

As he drove me to his village it was difficult to believe that it was a first-generation immigrant from Jamaica who was taking me through the English countryside, pointing out the village church which he attends, the pub nearby where a famous novel was written, and the Thames River winding through the wooded area, where he likes to walk his boxer dog. Everything seemed to be so English, and this impression was complete when we entered Henry's home, located in a small development of semi-detached houses, and his English wife welcomed us with tea and home-made cake. Henry seemed to defy any stereotyping of West Indians and to blend entirely with the English landscape. The seeds of his grounding in the English landscape were, however, sowed in Jamaica:

> I was from a family of eight, four boys and four girls. I was the fifth child. I went to school in [the local town] on the north coast of Jamaica, where I was born. Then I went to . . . High School. At 17 I worked at civil service in Jamaica, and at 18 I joined the RAF in Jamaica. We travelled to America, spent a month there and embarked from New York for Liverpool, England.

Long before joining the RAF and departing for Great Britain, Henry had been thoroughly inculcated with British culture and society:

culturally we were oriented toward England. All our laws and the government were English, the governor was from England, the troops were English, and there was a lot of English influence. The vicars were English, it is only in the later part of my life that Jamaicans and West Indians became priests, inspectors, MPs. Then Jamaica became independent in 1962.

. . .

A lot of the schools were run by English teachers, we knew more about the English history than the West Indian. Since I have grown up I have taken more interest in it.

For Henry, who grew up in a middle-class family in a regional administrative centre governed by representatives of the colonial regime, and who had finished his education at a private secondary school, British culture became an important and integral part of life. Thus, when he joined the RAF and went to England, he was not going to a foreign country, but to the old centre of the imperial culture which had suffused his early life. He saw no reason to seek out the company of other West Indians, but rather chose to mix with others:

When I joined the RAF at Abingdon, the captain said 'we have quite a bit of West Indians, would you like to live with them?' I said 'no, I will go where the trade takes me.' You should not try to be different, you should move along . . .

While he did experience some racial prejudice, he brushed it off as merely incidences of the kind of stereotyping which many others experience:

I have had racial abuses, but I took it in context. Somebody might yell 'bloody West Indian', but then he would also yell 'bloody Irishman', or 'bloody Welshman'. People do have a chip on their shoulder. When you are a minority there is a great feeling that you are being picked on. Of course it happens, and I would not deny that it happened. I am sure that even my children had problems because of me being their father, but they never brought it home to me. I always instilled in them to believe in their own self. They must stand on their own feet regardless. When you show yourself capable, eventually people will respect you. You must gain their respect, it goes a long way wherever you live, work, whatever you do.

Henry showed that he was capable and therefore he succeeded. This success, however, was not within the realm of material welfare or occupational prestige. When he had spent a year at a civil service job in England, after having left the RAF at the end of the war, he realized that it was a dead-end job offering little possibility of promotion and economic gain. He therefore took a job in welding and went to work on the production line in the motor industry. This job gave little 'job satisfaction', but he earned three–four times more money. It was still difficult for him to support his family when the children were small, and his wife did not work, and he readily acknowledged the help that he had received from his mother in Jamaica, who had put something for the children into her letters from Jamaica.

Henry's success derived from his ability to live as a respected member of English society. Here, he was able to capitalize on his competence as a cricket player, a game that he had learned to master in the Jamaican schools:

> People think that you are capable and ask if you will stand, and so I accept. From when I started my schooling I was captain of the cricket club in [the Jamaican] school. I was also captain of the cricket club [at an RAF station], and I even played in the Kennington Oval, the big venue for international cricket, when I was on the RAF cricket team. We played in the inter-station [RAF] final and we won.

This led to people asking him to assume other responsibilities within the field of cricket:

> I was chair of the [local] cricket club for 10 years. The chair runs the club, whereas the president is more of a figure head. I have played a lot of cricket for [my firm], played for them for about 12 years. I was also a representative on the pension fund for the last 15 years that I worked for them.

The cricket success paved the way for being asked to serve in other capacities not just at his work place, but also in the village where he lives. Thus he has been a member of the parish council for a number of years, and he and his wife are quite active in church life, participating in flower shows, fairs and so on.

Henry does not see his strong commitment to the local community, and to British culture and society in general, as being in conflict with his identity as a West Indian. He still regards Jamaica as his home, because he was born there, and he identifies himself as a Jamaican. Furthermore, his best friend throughout his life in England has been a fellow Jamaican who came to England with the RAF at the same time as Henry, and who lives in the area. This friend was best man at Henry's wedding and he still sees him socially. During his years as an active cricket player Henry also met many West Indians, who played for various local clubs, and socialized with them after the game. Furthermore, he had been invited to several exclusive small social gatherings to meet a cricket celebrity, and several of these celebrities had been West Indian. He emphasized, however, that he had never sought out people because they were West Indian, only because they were nice people, and when I asked him whether his life in England had been different in any way because of his West Indian background, he replied, 'Not at all!'

Social fields

It is noteworthy that two West Indians, whose occupational careers and levels of material success in England are fairly similar, should view their lives so differently. Both have been fully employed and performed skilled, physically demanding work throughout their long stay in England; both own their own homes in decent neighbourhoods, both are married and have successfully raised their children, and both have been active in their local communities, though these communities have been very different. Yet, Edwin was rather unhappy about the life which he had lived in England. He basically felt that he had been discriminated against in British society and was ready to return to Nevis as soon as he had the economic means to do so. Henry, on the other hand, expressed satisfaction with his achievements in life, despite the fact that he was not able to find a well-paying job that reflected his education, and he felt quite settled in the English community where he lived. The differences can, to a great extent, be accounted for by comparing the socio-economic background of the two, and the cultural orientation with which this background was associated.

Edwin grew up in a poor, rural village of small farmers and plantation labourers and he never finished elementary school, because he wished to take gainful employment so that he would no longer be a burden on his parents who had a large family to support. He noted, himself, that an important reason why he, and many of his friends from Nevis and other West Indian islands, had become so disappointed about their life in England was that they had known very little about the country and had unrealistic expectations:

We had heard fantastic stories about England, like how money was growing on trees in the back yard, and all you had to do was shake the tree and the money would fall down. Or the streets were paved with gold. People were very disappointed when they came here. They thought that the English were the godliest, most honest and righteous people on earth. When I grew up there was little contact with English people. There was not even a dozen white people on Nevis and they were very isolated, lived at places like [the estate and hotel] Mt Pellier, where Black people could not afford to go. So we were overjoyed to go to England, it was a great thing, it was the next best to going to heaven.

Edwin's lack of exposure to English people and their way of life made him seek the company of his own people. Thus, he left Oxford as soon as possible to move to a community of West Indians, many of them friends from Nevis, where he might feel 'at home'. For Edwin, England therefore turned out to be essentially a foreign and uncomfortable place, because the sentiments which he nourished towards England were based on a kind of imagining which had little to do with actual life in England.

Henry was in an entirely different situation. He grew up in a colonial administrative centre, where he had socialized with English people. Furthermore, he had completed secondary education, spoke 'proper' English and had a fair amount of knowledge about English culture when he left for England. This, combined with his very light complexion, which meant that he did not particularly stand out in a crowd of white Englishmen, as Edwin did, meant that it was relatively easy for him to mix in British society. And he made it a point of doing exactly this. Thus, he chose not to be boarded with West Indians when it hindered him from becoming part of a British institution, and he capitalized on his ability to play cricket and on his 'cultured' and educated background, both learned in the West Indies, when it helped him gain respect and, hence, acceptance in the local community.

I would contend, however, that Edwin's and Henry's life stories also must be seen in the light of the continued importance of the wider, non-local family networks of the two men – though in entirely different ways. In Edwin's case this resulted in a rather pessimistic outlook, whereas in the case of Henry, it led to a highly positive tone. I interviewed Edwin – not very long after the death of his parents and the resultant inheritance of the family home, which they had owned and occupied, by a sister who had remained in the home with them and cared for them. With the sister as the sole owner of the house, Edwin had, in essence, lost the firm anchoring point to which he had returned during his visits on the island. This was particularly the case, because the siblings, as noted, could not agree on how to divide the land. Edwin explained that his father had offered the entire piece of land to him because he was the eldest son, but that he had turned down the offer. He had done this because he felt that all the siblings had helped the parents by sending remittances or staying behind and caring for them, and everybody therefore ought to have a share in the land. Now he was beginning to regret this decision, being left with no land at all, as the siblings differed about how to divide it. The feeling of alienation and discrimination which Edwin evoked to characterize his life in British society, and the unfriendly welcome which he described receiving on Nevis as a British returnee, thus was heightened by the fact that he had lost the firm source of identification and belonging which his parents, their home and land, and the wider family network had constituted for him. The fact that the land had become a site of contention and strife, and that he had been shown no respect as the eldest son, had become particularly troublesome for Edwin, and he was worried about his imminent trip to Nevis where he would see his siblings again, saying: 'I still love them, but I have this sadness about it.' He was conscious of the psychological effect this family crisis was having upon him, and he told me that he had now become interested in religion and begun to study with the Jehovah's Witnesses in order to find out about what had happened to his parents after their death.

When I interviewed Henry, he had just had a week-long visit from his brother, who had had a successful career in a major corporation in New York. The meeting of the family, which had taken place the previous year at a sister's funeral in New York, was also fresh in his mind. Furthermore, he was well aware that I was going to interview most of his relatives in the United States, Canada and the West Indies. All this led him to relate his life story in contrastive terms *vis-à-vis* the sort of life that he might have had, had he left for the United States, as had several of his brothers and sisters. Such a life might have been his, but fate made it otherwise, and he was just as glad. He explained that as a youngster he had actually applied for a visa to go to the United States, but it took so long for the papers to come that he opted instead to join the RAF and go to Great Britain. Two weeks later the American papers arrived:

> I have no regrets about it. I have had a happy life. I might have been materially better off, but not morally. I have been satisfied with the

life I have lived. I would not have had the lovely wife and children and grandchildren. It was destiny, and I have no regrets.

The high moral quality, which he attributed to his life, rested to a great extent on the superiority which he attached to life in Great Britain as compared to that which he experienced during his visits in the United States. His ability to mix in British society, and become part of the local community, derived from the lack of discrimination which he experienced in British society:

> I mix freely in the community, and I am not sure whether this would be the case in America. There is no type of discrimination in the local area where I live. You get that from the respect that you have gained from people. You must achieve that respect where you are, it should not matter who you are . . .

But also in terms of more general cultural values and ways of acting he preferred the British way:

> I am very pro-British. On the whole I find the American way of life very cosmetic, over-reacting to most things, everything is bigger than big, and when it comes to the crunch to show your metal they are not there.

His emphasis on mixing, gaining respect in the local community and upholding moral virtues, which he associated with good, British values, therefore should not just be read as an account of a happy life in Great Britain. It should also be interpreted as a counter narrative to the sort of narratives which he expected his North American family to relate about occupational achievements and economic affluence.

Conclusion

In a contribution to a recent book on Caribbean migration, the British sociologist Robin Cohen notes: 'Migration scholars – normally a rather conservative breed of sociologists, historians, demographers and geographers – have recently been bemused to find their subject matter assailed by a bevy of postmodernists, novelists and scholars of cultural studies. A reconstitution of the notion of diaspora has been a central concern of these space invaders' (R. Cohen 1998: 21). Cohen goes on to examine whether there really is such a thing as a Caribbean cultural diaspora and concludes that a 'more solid and accurate understanding of the nature' of this diaspora 'will only be possible by gathering full historical information and sociological data' (ibid.: 33). While such information will undoubtedly be very useful, I have here argued that a closer attention to the analytical framework, which the 'diasporic' approach implies, is perhaps a more indispensable task. I have here questioned whether the notion of diaspora, a displaced community of belonging and identification rooted in a temporally and geographically distant homeland, can take us very far in studies of the lives which migrants have carved out for themselves and the sort of understanding of these lives which they have developed.

Through an examination of two life stories related by people who have been involved in migratory movements, I have argued that the communities which emerge at the individual level of imagining are difficult to explore in their full complexity by subsuming them under the general heading of diaspora. Both life stories might be characterized as having diasporic dimensions – both, for example, described their West Indian island of origin as home and identified themselves as nationals of their West Indian homeland. The West Indian homelands, which the two narrators imagined for themselves, were entirely different, however, and they led to very different cultural identities. It might be tempting to argue that the difference in cultural identification was due to the fact that Edwin, who had been a keen member of the Caribbean community in Leeds, had maintained strong ties to the Caribbean, whereas Henry, who had settled in an English village, basically had become English and lost touch with his Caribbean background. This interpretation is not warranted because both very much identified with, and acted in accordance with, their Caribbean cultural background. Their cultural background in the Caribbean, however, was quite dissimilar with Edwin being grounded in a rather isolated community of African-Caribbean small farmers and fishermen, Henry in a parish capital strongly imbued with British colonial culture. Differing Caribbean backgrounds therefore provided them with different vantage points from which to establish themselves as Caribbean people in Great Britain. With his middle-class background in English colonial culture, Henry found in cricket and the Anglican Church natural avenues of acceptance into the white, English society with which he was already well versed in Jamaica. With his lower-class background in African–Caribbean culture, Edwin chose to establish himself as a respected member of the local Caribbean community by excelling in dominoes and being active in organizations working for the improvement of this community in British society. The very different senses of Caribbeanness expressed by these two men therefore call into question the general tendency in migration studies to treat people as categories of persons, who can be classified according to places of origin.

While Edwin's and Henry's understanding, and practice, of Caribbean culture were related to their disparate social and cultural backgrounds in the Caribbean, which offered them different vantage points from which to establish themselves in Great Britain, their experiences of migrating and settling in Great Britain were also strongly mediated by the global fields of family relations of which they were part. Thus, it was apparent that the life stories that Edwin and Henry related were part of ongoing conversations, maintained through phone calls, letters and visits within their widely dispersed family networks. These networks therefore constituted narrative communities of close, interpersonal relations where moral values, social relations and cultural identities were continuously constructed and reconstructed through stories. These globally circulated stories reflected the common background in the Caribbean and the family home there shared by all family members, as well as the various local contexts within which different individuals were situated. Individuals therefore did not just imagine their place, cultural identity or home in the Caribbean, they also experienced them through concrete and intimate relations with family members, and the narrative communities that they constituted. These experiences, in turn, had an important bearing on the ways in which individuals interpreted and imagined the more abstract and generalized categories of being Nevisian, Jamaican or English. By examining stories of dispersal, locality and belonging, and the narrative communities that these stories nourish and sustain, we may therefore be able to explore the significance of individuality in migrant communities, while, at the same time, recognizing the importance of wider communities of belonging and identification.

Notes

1 This chapter is a revised version of a paper presented at the workshop 'Community revisited: A review of the relationship between community, place and culture' at the European Association of Social Anthropologists' Biannual Meeting in Frankfurt, 1998. The chapter has benefited from the discussion at the workshop. I would like to thank Vered Amit, in particular, for her helpful comments on the chapter.

2 In her useful discussion of transnationalism Sarah Mahler has noted, 'Much of the research to date on transnational social fields yields detailed information on a limited set of activities and practices, not a clear picture of the breath of the social field, nor of the demography or intensity of players' participation in all the activities people engage in. A prime example is the

important treatise, *Nations Unbound*, by Linda Basch, Cristina Szanton Blanc and Nina Glick Schiller (1992). This book begins with a framework for researching transnationalism in a broad sense, but the ethnographic work cited is focused on voluntary associations and political campaigns' (1998: 82).

3 This research has been sponsored by the Danish Research Council of Development Research and is part of a larger ongoing research programme *Livelihood, Identity and Organization in Situations of Instability*. This support is gratefully appreciated. I also wish to thank the members of the family networks for helping me with the research.

4 In order to protect the anonymity of the family members I have changed their names.

References

Anderson, Benedict (1983) *Imagined Communities: Reflections on the Origins and Spread of Nationalism*. London: Verso.

Appadurai, Arjun (1996) *Modernity at Large: Cultural Dimensions of Globalisation*. Minneapolis: University of Minnesota Press.

Basch, Linda, Nina Glick Schiller and Cristina Szanton Blanc (1993) *Nations Unbound: Transnational Projects, Postcolonial Predicaments and Deterritorialized Nation-States*. Basel: Gordon and Breach.

Cohen, Anthony P. (1982) 'Belonging: The Experience of Culture', in A. P. Cohen (ed.) *Belonging, Identity and Social Organisation in British Rural Cultures*. Manchester: Manchester University Press, pp. 1–17.

—— (1996) 'Personal Nationalism: A Scottish View of some Rites, Rights, and Wrongs'. *American Ethnologist* 23(4): 802–15.

Cohen, Robin (1998) 'Cultural Diasporas: The Caribbean Case,' in Mary Chamberlain (ed.) *Caribbean Migration: Globalised Identities*. London: Routledge, pp. 21–35.

Ekman, Ann-Kristin (1991) *Community, Carnival and Campaign: Expressions of Belonging in a Swedish Region*. Stockholm Studies in Anthropology no. 2.

Gullestad, Marianne (1994) 'Constructions of Self and Society in Autobiographical Accounts: A Scandinavian Life Story', in Eduardo P. Archetti (ed.) *Exploring the Written: Anthropology and the Multiplicity of Writing*. Oslo: Scandinavian University Press, pp. 123–63.

Kearney, M. (1995) 'The Local and the Global: The Anthropology of Globalisation and Transnationalism'. *Annual Review of Anthropology* 24: 547–65.

Mahler, Sarah (1998) 'Theoretical and Empirical Contributions Toward a Research Agenda for Transnationalism', in M. P. Smith and L. E. Guarnizo (eds) *Transnationalism from Below*. New Brunswick: Transaction Publishers, pp. 64–100.

Ochs, Elinor and Lisa Capps (1996) 'Narrating the Self'. *Annual Review in Anthropology* 25: 19–43.

Olwig, Karen (1997) 'Toward a Reconceptualization of Migration and

Transnationalism', in Bodil Folke Frederiksen and Fiona Wilson (eds) *Livelihood, Identity and Instability*. Copenhagen: Centre for Development Research, pp. 113–27.

Peacock, James L. and Dorothy C. Holland (1993) 'The Narrated Self: Life Stories in Process'. *Ethos* 21(4): 367–83.

Rapport, Nigel (1993) *Diverse World-Views in an English Village*. Edinburgh: University of Edinburgh Press.

——(1997) *Transcendent Individual: Towards a Literary and Liberal Anthropology*. London: Routledge.

Schiller, Nina Glick, Linda Basch and Cristina Szanton Blanc (eds) (1992) *Toward a Transnational Perspective on Migration*. New York: The New York Academy of Sciences

Somers, Margaret R. (1994) 'The Narrative Constitution of Identity: A Relational and Network Approach'. *Theory and Society* 23: 605–49.

Strathern, Marilyn (1982) 'The Village as an Idea: Constructs of Village-ness in Elmdon, Essex', in A. P. Cohen (ed.) *Belonging, Identity and Social Organisation in British Rural Cultures*. Manchester: Manchester University Press, pp. 247–77.

Chapter 8

Post-cultural anthropology
The ironization of values in a world of movement

Nigel Rapport

> We need an anthropology which does not make a fetish of culture . . .
> Our predicament is – to work out the social options of our affluent
> and disenchanted condition. We have no choice about this.
>
> (Ernest Gellner *Anthropology and Politics*)

Introduction: Nietzsche, Gellner, Forster

In his discussion on the best possible relationship between science and
non-science (in which he included religion and the arts), Nietzsche
decided on the image of human beings having 'a double brain', a brain
with two chambers lying next to one another, as it were, separable and
self-contained, and experiencing different things without confusion
(1994: 154). An experience of both science and non-science was necessary for human health, Nietzsche deemed, but at the same time the two
had to be kept apart. Non-science inspired and was the source of human
strength, while science was the source of truth, direction and regulation;
while non-science gave rise to those illusions, errors, fantasies and pas-
sions by which human life was heated, scientific knowledge served to
protect from the pernicious consequences of overheating. If not for non-
science, scientific truths would eventually seem commonplace and
everyday, and lose their charm; if not for science and the continuing
search for truth, the joys of non-science would cause 'higher culture' to
'relapse into barbarism' (1994: 154).

At first blush, Nietzsche's language and his conclusions seem distinctly 'non-anthropological', as disciplinary dispensations commonly
delineate that term today. However, Ernest Gellner, shortly before he
died, came to advocate propositions strikingly similar to Nietzsche's. A
culture, Gellner suggested, is a collectivity united in a belief: '[m]ore particularly, a collectivity united in a false belief is a culture' (1995a: 6). For

what is particular to a culture is its errors, and commitment to these comes to define a community of faith as a badge of loyalty and belonging (1995a: 6):

> Assent to an absurdity identifies an intellectual *rite de passage*, a gateway to the community defined by that commitment to that conviction.

Truth, meanwhile, that which is disinterred by science, is available to all and valid for all. Science represents a form of knowledge, a cognitive style and an understanding of nature which reaches beyond any one culture so as to transform totally the terms of reference in which human societies operate. Science offers propositions and claims which can be translated, without loss of efficacy, into any socio-cultural milieu, and whose application, as technology, provides a means universally of transforming the human condition.

However, science alone is also insufficient. Gellner calls it 'too thin, too abstract, too far removed from the earthy and the concrete' to support most people in a crisis (1995b: 7); it may correctly give on to what is, but it does not 'warm the heart, or help a man sustain a tragedy, or behave with dignity when circumstances become too much for him' (1995b: 8). In Weberian terms, the triumph of rationality enables a more efficient satisfaction of human wants, but it also drains social life of the mystification necessary to afford efficiency any meaning beyond itself. While science has changed the traditional habit of employing religious doctrine to underwrite our values, then, it can offer little in its place; continually changing itself, scientific knowledge of the world can be expected to furnish few foundations by which rigid moral prescriptions might be legitimated. This spells moral crisis.

What is needed, Gellner concludes, is a healthy admixture or amalgam of scientific order and truth, on the one hand, and cultural, moral community and faith, on the other. Gellner's (half-serious) image is of a 'constitutional religion' (1993: 91), run on a similar basis to a constitutional monarchy, which underwrites community, which retains the ritual and symbolism of an earlier non-scientific age, but is now deprived of real power in its relationship to social life; this runs instead along instrumental and profane lines. Religious institutions may mirror the past only, not the present situation of decision-making, but the non-scientific idiom continues to afford social legitimation, aestheticism and comfort in ways which the realities of scientific knowledge do not.

I would describe Gellner's notion of a constitutional religion as only half-serious because I believe he felt humankind could do better. It could better approach the goal of securing agreement on principles of justice which allowed for the peaceful coexistence in one liberal polity of persons with divergent, even incommensurable, conceptions of the good life and worldview. (Of course, many of the participants in the political debate over 'civil society' and the engendering of a 'constitutional faith' (Hugo Black), a 'Verfassungspatriotismus' (Habermas) hope so too.) Gellner, moreover, felt that anthropology had a significant role to play in the process. For a start, anthropology could seek an answer as to why scientific knowledge was so successful with regard to the domains of nature and technology, but not to others, such as culture and morality.

Science proved that knowledge beyond culture was possible; indeed, Gellner referred to this as '*the* fact of our lives' (1993: 54), and the starting point of any adequate anthropological appreciation of our shared, global, human condition today:

> Our world is indeed a plural one, but it is based on the uniqueness of truth, on the astonishing technological power of one particular cognitive style, namely science and its application.
>
> (1995b: 3)

But if knowledge was global in this way, then why not morality? If '[v]alid knowledge ignores and does not engender frontiers' (1995a: 6), then may not anthropology work towards the formulation of a morality similarly beyond community and the particularities of culture? Granted that a symbolic domain alongside the technical one of science may continue to be necessary for human comfort, but could not this domain likewise assume globalism and be ultimately subject to reason? Certainly, Gellner thought this *the* necessary anthropological project, however difficult, practically, such moral arrangements might be to set up.

The liberal societies of the West Gellner called 'well-matured political systems'; here (echoes of a 'constitutional religion'), 'absolutist symbols, shorn of too much power, coexist amicably with pragmatic, effective powers shorn of too much symbolic potency' (1995b: 9). However, more needed to be done and better could be accrued; human liberty deserved surer foundations than the purely technological and commercial workings of the 'McWorld' – McDonalds, Macintosh computers and MTV music (Barber 1996: 140). In the contemporary West, science sat alongside morality (usually in the form of religion or relativism) courtesy of an uneasy relationship of ambiguity. A balance was achieved between the moral 'thinness' of science, on the one hand, and the moral rigidity of religion and the tolerance of relativism, on the other hand, by no-one having to declare his (*or her*) loyalties clearly or finally (to himself or to others); a person could vacillate between science and non-science according to circumstance without being pressured into selecting one option over the other. However, the relationship was also unstable. Certainly, if the model was to be copied elsewhere on the globe (such as the post-Communist East), and if it was itself to be protected from adverse developments elsewhere on the globe (such as the reactionary fundamentalisms of the Middle East), then it needed clarifying and stiffening. A global morality alongside a global science, to repeat, might be expected to share a certain rationality and hence to be mutually supportive, even if remaining different in cognitive style . . .

Gellner seemed to like ending paragraphs with three dots (. . .) which suggested at once a following-on and a lack of ending. They also bring to my mind flow and movement. I read into them a *movement* into the future, when anthropology starts to tackle the socio-cultural issues of a world of *movement* (a flow of people, goods, behavioural forms and ideas around the globe), by way of a set of propositions which afford a *movement* between scientific knowledge and morality. How, in short, might one move from the world of material security and individual liberty, to which the Enlightenment project of scientific investigation has given rise, to a world of rational morality in which all may have faith, all may feel they belong, all may find beauty, comfort, solace and security? While not presuming to provide a definitive response, in this essay, I wish to take Gellner's questions and his project for anthropology seriously; I want to formulate an anthropological account, descriptive and prescriptive, of interaction in a 'post-cultural world' of science, migration, irony and individuality, of global morality, civil society and human rights.

I also want to move towards an answer by thinking in terms of movement: truth as movement as means for coming to terms with the truth of a world of movement. But E. M. Forster has said it far better than me:

> The business man who assumes that life is everything, and the mystic who asserts that it is nothing, fail on this side and on that, to hit the truth. 'Yes, I see dear, it's about half-way between,' Aunt Juley had hazarded in earlier years. No: truth, being alive, was not half-way between anything. It was only to be found *by continuous excursions into either realm*, and though proportion is the final secret, to espouse it at the outset is to ensure sterility [my emphasis].

This is extracted from the novel *Howards End* (1950: 174), and I am struck by the appositeness for the discussion here of Forster's notion of truth as 'alive', as movement, as a balance and as phenomenological or existential. To 'hit on the truth' entails a process of juxtaposing erstwhile separate sets of information and domains of knowledge, and cognitively bringing them together so that their differences connect. But importantly, this connection does not take the form of a common denomination or generalization, of finding a middle way between. Rather, separate things are kept separate, their integrity respected, and it is only the perceiver who, undertaking an experiential journey into the realms of each and coming to an understanding of each in its own terms, then brings these understandings together in the mind for comparison and collation. These separate understandings never merge into a static synthetic state, never coalesce into a *tertium quid*; for they are ever derived from and maintained by opposition. And hence the truth continues to be 'alive', and remains something to be found in moving from one understanding to another.

In what Forster says I find significant possible correspondences with both Nietzsche and Gellner; (besides the novel, *Howards End*, Forster also makes use of the imagery of achieving proportion in essays such as 'What I Believe' (1972) where tolerance, good temper and sympathy must be amalgamated with faith, as he sees it, if they are to be stiffened sufficiently to withstand the advances of the many more 'militant creeds' likely to beset them). Science and morality (religion, culture and the arts) represent two distinct domains of human experience, both phenomenologically vital. However, equally vital is that they be somehow brought together and interrelated if human social life in community is to be blessed with, and benefit from, both knowledge of reality and pleasure in reality. The way to bring them together, moreover, is not fusion or synthesis, but by their common individual experiencing and by the writing of a cognitive narrative whereby one continually moves from the experience of one to that of the other.

What Forster and Nietzsche and Gellner all look forward to is knowledge of those socio-cultural circumstances in which individuals are prone habitually to make such a journey. It is a question of displacement.

The ironization of liberal democracy

Nietzsche described a 'revaluation of all values' as his formula for humankind's supreme 'coming-to-itself'. The cognitive act which he called for was an ironic one; the human quality he was calling upon, and raising into a supreme value itself, was irony. Besides its literary meaning, of certain figures of speech (antiphrasis, litotes, meiosis) where there is an inconsistency or contradiction between what is said and what is meant or apparent, irony can be understood as compassing a certain cognitive detachment; it is the recognition of a displacement. Indeed, irony might be defined as the royal road to appreciating displacement as an infinite regress.

Irony may be defined (ironically) as: 'never having to say you really mean it' (Austin-Smith 1990: 51–2), or never accepting that words mean only what they seem to say. Treated more broadly, I would include in its definition, first, an ontological premise that individuals may never be cognitively imprisoned by seemingly pre-ordained and pre-determining schema of cultural classification and social structuration. For, second, and existentially, individuals can everywhere appreciate the malleability and the mutability of all social rules and realities, and the contingency and ambiguity of cultural truths. Hence, third, and descriptively, individuals may always practise a certain detachment from the world as it is for the purpose of imagining alternatives. In unmasking the world as an ambiguous fiction, irony plays with the possibility of limitless alterity. Here is an ability and a practice, enduring and ubiquitous, by which individuals may loose themselves from the security of what is or appears to be and creatively explore what might be. Here is a process by which human beings may render even the most cherished of their values, beliefs and desires open to question, parody and replacement. However momentary the impulse, irony represents a celebration of the fictive nature of all such human inheritances and the imaging of other worlds.

George Kateb (1984) is careful to avoid positing a one-to-one relationship between type of socio-cultural milieu and type of individual cognition and way of experiencing; there was no saying that the ironic perspective associated with democratic individuality was a way of being in the world particular to liberal democracy. It was rather that under the latter conditions, ironization was legally recognized and constitutionally enlisted. For others, however, the ironical stance or attitude is something historically and culturally specific. Ortega (1956), for instance, suggests that the ability to become detached from the immediacy of the world and treat it ironically is a manifestation of the technological revolution in human civilization. Entering an intense, inner world in which ideas are formed which are then returned to the world as a blueprint for its re-construction represents a concentration which humankind has created for itself painfully and slowly. The growth of irony has followed a growth in science, and the freedom not to be obliged inexorably to concern oneself with reacting to things as they are, but temporarily to ignore the latter in favour of a created self and a plan of action. In short, irony as that detachment by which the world becomes anthropomorphized, a reflection and realization of human ideas, is a technological by-product.

Oppenheimer (1989), meanwhile, attaches an ironic consciousness to certain literary forms. Irony was present in Socratic dialogue, then, and also in the poetics of classical Rome, but thereafter, through some seven centuries of the Dark Ages, it disappeared. Only with the rise of the sonnet in Rome of the twelfth century was there an ironic renaissance. The sonnet might be described, therefore, as the lyric of 'personality' and the 'private soul', for with its invention came a new way for people to think as and about themselves. Irony, as we presently appreciate it, is a matter of that introspection and self-consciousness which the possible silent reading of the sonnet literary form made fashionable, conventional, esteemed, and hence possible.

Finally, Giddens (1990) would make an argument that only modernity, that recent sociological condition characterized by capitalism, industrialism, cosmopolitanism and the massification of complex society, is characterized by an ironic detachment. Indeed, the presumption of this reflexivity – including our sociological reflection upon our reflexivity – is an intrinsic part of modern social practice. We constantly examine and reform our practices in the light of incoming information about those practices, which thus alters the character and constitution of the practices we next examine. Irony, in short, is part-and-parcel of the process of structuration by which modernity reproduces itself and knows itself.

Notwithstanding the above, I am convinced that the cognitive displacement and detachment of irony is a universal human trait, capacity and cognitive resort. As John Berger sums up the case (1994):

> [T]he human condition actually is more or less a constant: always in face of the same mysteries, the same dilemmas, the same temptation to despair, and always armed unexpectedly with the same energy.

Or, in more strictly anthropological vein:

> [T]here were never any innocent, unconscious savages, living in a time of unreflective and instinctive harmony. We human beings are all and always sophisticated, conscious, capable of laughter at our own institutions.
>
> (Turner, in Ashley 1990: xix)

This is the ground of anthropology: . . . We can pretend that . . . the people we are studying are living amid various unconscious systems of determining forces of which they have no clue and to which only we have the key. But it is only pretence.

(Rabinow 1977: 151–2)

Always and everywhere one finds 'individuals engaged in the creative exploration of culture' (Goody 1977: 20), intellectually distancing themselves from the existing conceptual universe and looking at it askance. Always and everywhere, individuals are prone and able to 'detach themselves', to question the value and justification of the roles and practices in which they are currently implicated, and to envision themselves with different relationships and preferences. Any notion of a binary divide between those (intellectual individuals, times and places) with irony and those without, Goody concludes, is a nonsense.

An extended endorsement of this position is provided by Handler and Segal's (1990) examination of the writings of Jane Austen. Writing in, and of, a time and society (early nineteenth-century England) where irony might seem a far cry from a conventionally stable, unambiguous, axiomatic and homogeneous way of life, Austen shows no ironic 'reticence'. Readily ironizing any claims of a seemingly integrated and bounded socio-cultural system to give on to a singular or unitary truth, she affords an appreciation of the normative, the institutional and the principled in culture (here, the implicit cultural principles of genteel English society of marriage, courtship, rank and gender) as symbolic forms always subject to, and needful of, creative interpretation: to independent manipulation and individual re-rendering. Handler and Segal dub it 'alter-cultural action'. Clearly, for Austen, the schema of cultural classification and social structuration, being arbitrary, and being recognized to be arbitrary, may be seen less to regulate conduct or ensure the unconscious reproduction of an established order than to give communicative resource, significance and value to what Handler and Segal describe as her characters' 'serious social play'. Rather than norms which are taken literally, conventional etiquette and propriety become matters for metacommunicative comment and analysis – and hence are displaced – in the process of individual constructions of situational socio-cultural order.

In short, the writings of Jane Austen are a celebration of the 'fiction of culture' and individuals' creative potential for alter-cultural world-making: of the enduring human disposition to render all socio-cultural norms ultimately contingent. Furthermore, what is true for Austen's language is true for language as such: it is 'of its very nature, an ironic mode' (Martin 1983: 415), imbued with the multiple ironies of there being no certain or necessary accordance between the linguistic meanings of different individuals, or between those and the way the world is. And what is true for Austen's age is true for all times. Hutcheon notes (1994: 9) that the historical claim to be an 'age of irony' is a repeated one, but perhaps equally or more true is its denial; for the social milieux in which the cognitive freedom (scepticism, creativity, idiosyncrasy) which irony flags, the will and the practice to complexify, multiply and call into question socio-cultural realities, is welcomed are at least balanced by a blinkered absolutism or fundamentalism in which the substance of inherited verities alone is validated. But whether it is celebrated or negated on the level of public convention, irony exists as a cognitive proclivity and practice, embodying a certain imaginative movement from the world(s) as is, a certain reflection upon the latter and differentiation from it.

Of course, not all such cognitive movements, reflections and differentiations need be identified as ironic. Irony amounts to cognitive movement as an endemic mode of being; it represents, as I said, something of a royal road to recognizing infinite displacement and regress, infinite revaluation of values. Certain other cognitions partake of part of this movement, but not its habituation. Conversion, for instance, can be said to entail a cognitive shift or move such that one looks back at a position from which one has now become displaced – from which one has displaced oneself – due to an original sense of 'meaning-deficit' in one's life and a need for revitalization (Fernandez 1995: 22). However, this does not amount to displacement as an ongoing cognitive resort, as a conscious way of being: to being as an endemic becoming. And yet, this latter seems to be essential to irony; it is a living with displacement, and a refusing to take any value as absolute, as free from revaluation, except the value of revaluation *per se*.

E. M. Forster was once described as having a 'whim of iron' (Trilling 1951: 11), refusing to take anything too seriously, too conclusively, too fixedly, except the proclivity to reconsider, to change and move on, as such. In arguing on behalf of self-reliance, meanwhile, Emerson (1981) felt that ongoing self-examination, a continual distancing of oneself from one's self, instilled an inner iron whereby an individual could withstand the descriptions others made of him, and so go on thinking his own thought. A self-examined self is set at a distance from the immediacies of present experience and thus is kept safe from presentist critique. It is removed from the seeming sacredness of extant traditions and engaged with what is ultimately sacred: the integrity of its own mind. The self-reliant, self-distant individual lives from within and belongs to no particular time or place: he is his own centre; his nature, his mind, is its own measure. 'Every true man is a cause, a country, an age . . . Where he is, there is nature' (Emerson 1981: 148, 147).

If Emerson's Romantic language sounds dated (in need of being taken ironically), then this should not detract from its truth. There is an individual capacity to transcend present ontologies and epistemologies, present appearances, and insist on the reality of its own being and becoming. Irony is part-and-parcel of this individual force which 'insists on itself' and proceeds continually to create and to live its own truth. Moreover, this is a continuous process because every truth reached is recognized to be contingent and perspectival, and bound to be left behind in a progression of meaning which is without limit.

Human rights and liberal democracy

If the individual who ironically resists the temptation to cherish particular values, beliefs and desires over and above their continuing revaluation is existentially free, then, as Kateb demonstrates (1981; 1991), he can still be greatly helped by certain legal-constitutional arrangements, by the procedures of a liberal democracy, which recognize and champion that free ironism. The exercise of ironism benefits from the legalism of 'human rights' which 'allow for the free exercise of choice as to [the individual's] involvements and protect against unreflective, herd solidarity' (Phillips 1993: 191).

Human rights, in the past fifty years, has become 'one of the most globalised political values of our times' (Wilson 1997: 1). And yet, most anthropological literature has isolated itself from mainstream discussion. It has tended to regard the legalistic language and the institutional frameworks of much discussion of rights as falling outside its professional scope (cf. Messer 1993), and questions of better or worse practices as value-judgements which go against its professional ethos. While 'human rights', as discourse and as international law, has enjoyed enormous growth, anthropology has remained relativistically aloof, if not sceptical.

Even when they have found themselves, perforce, within the human rights arena, anthropologists have been loath to pass judgement on what might be meant by such notions as the right to life, to adequate food, shelter, health care and education, to privacy and the ownership of property, to freedom from slavery and genocide, to freedom of movement, to freedom of speech, religion and assembly. Even practices such as female circumcision (clitoridectomy and infibulation), anthropologists have insisted, must needs be treated as a 'problem' by those affected before cultural outsiders may intervene and provide information for change; for 'rights' only exist when claimed or perceived within a society as a particular cultural form. Little wonder that, as Wilson puts it, anthropology is often viewed by human-rights' theorists and activists as 'the last bastion of cultural absolutism' (1997: 3): some Romantic reaction to the Enlightenment cult of progress (Gellner 1995b: 95).

This stance may be regarded as anachronistic, if not irresponsible and reactionary. In a 'post-cultural' world (Wilson again), a world where '[t]he "fantasy" that humanity is divided into [discrete groups] with clear frontiers of language and culture seems finally to be giving way to notions of disorder and openness', anthropologists often remain committed to a romantic communitarianism and relativism (Wilson 1997: 10). They continue to believe that, as canonized by the 1947 statement of the American Anthropological Association executive board (penned chiefly by Melville Herskovits), it is upon 'a respect for cultural differences' that respect for all other social and individual differences should be based (1947: 541). (On this view, cultures contain an inherent moral rectitude – such that one might always expect 'underlying cultural values' ultimately to assuage immoral political systems (ibid.: 543).)

Human rights and anthropological relativism

Inasmuch as anthropology has seen its pedagogic mission as the furtherance of respect for 'other cultures' – argued for the rights to cultural difference, and posited cultural differences as the grounds for all others – it can be seen to have adopted a collectivist and relativistic ethos.

The thinking behind anthropological relativism is well rehearsed (cf. Downing and Kushner 1988). Equally well rehearsed are the arguments against relativistic thinking. It has morally nihilistic, politically conservative and quietist consequences; the noble goal of understanding others in their own terms slips into a legitimation of inegalitarian and repressive political regimes and facilitates acquiescence to state repression. Indeed, if groups really possess complete moral autonomy then none can be criticized by members of another. Non-Westerners cannot criticize Western colonialism, and non-Muslims cannot criticize a religious death-warrant against a British novelist (the 'Salman Rushdie Affair') – both being products of cultural logics. International charities and aid agencies have no right to operate proactively, and there is no way justifiably to operationalize one's revulsion against slavery, female circumcision, gas chambers or gulags, or any other form of intolerant illiberalism or totalitarianism.

Inasmuch as many of the cultural groupings whose practices relativists would seek to defend are themselves far from relativistic or respecters of diversity, whether internal or externally, the relativist perforce commits a sin at second-hand: he endorses anti-relativism. Indeed, if no overriding values and criteria for judgement can be posited outwith cultural groups, if truth only exists internally to a culture and its norms, and diversity is 'terminal', then there is no place for the relativist to articulate his own position concerning cultural sovereignty; human commonalities must be claimed if only to defend the universal rights of cultural difference, and to explain and describe this diversity at the outset.

Looked at empirically, bridges have always been built between cultures, throughout history, and individuals have always refused to be constrained in their choices by their groups' conceptual boundaries and systems. Indeed, it is often today the so-called beneficiaries of cultural distinctiveness who most want to be rid of what keeps them from exercising the choices they see others enjoying. 'What is this "culture" concept?', the anthropologist-cum-refugee-administrator Lisa Gilad reports being often asked at immigration offices in Canada, and 'What about my rights as an individual woman?' Why do we maintain the anthropological stereotype that individualist thinking and social criticism are Western prerogatives and are not as firmly rooted in tribal milieux (cf. Burridge 1979), in Islam (cf. Amin 1989), or in Japan (cf. Macfarlane 1992)? As Gilad concludes, 'What, then, about the obligations of communities and states to their individual members?', 'What about respect for these latter?' (1996: 82–3). In short, arguments for cultural relativism are logically inconsistent: inevitably imbued with a number of inconsistencies and a self-contradicting meta-narrative (cf. Gellner 1993).

Culturally relativist arguments also imply a modelling of society and of culture which many (including Gellner, as we have heard) would now describe as outmoded. That is, society and culture are depicted as *sui generis*: as reified and as ontologically secure. They are modelled as entities, not processes: hermetically bounded and discrete; internally integrated, orderly and homogeneous; the basis of all similarities and differences between people, the ground of their being, the bank of their knowledge. This illusion of holism might have been legitimate currency in nineteenth-century nationalism and in Durkheimian sociology, but it is of little account in contemporary existential contexts of globalization:

of synchronicity, hybridity and creolization. Mechanistic, social-structural notions of society and culture as organically functioning and evolving wholes must now give way to existential notions of human groupings as purposive political entities (ethnicities, religiosities, localisms, occupational lobbies) which live on as sets of symbols and interpreted meanings in the minds of their members. As Wilson sums up, 'bounded conceptions of linguistic and cultural systems' are out of place in a context where culture may be characterized as 'contested, fragmented, contextualised and emergent' (1997: 9); where the more appropriate watchwords are chaos, entropy, multiplicity, inconsistency, contradiction, unpredictability and muddling-through (cf. Rapport 1997).

'Culture', in this situation, may not be raised as a right-bearing entity over and against human individuals. Individuals may have rights to cultural attachment and belonging and rights to membership of one or more cultures (of their choosing), but cultures do not have rights over individuals or members. On this view, female circumcision is a violation of: (a) the right to freedom from physical and psychological abuse; (b) the right to health and education; and (c) the right to corporal and sexual integrity (Boulware-Miller 1985: 155–77). More generally, the noble anthropological goal of seeking to understand others in their own terms cannot be employed as an excuse to avoid making moral and ethical judgements. Individuals have the right to resist and opt out of the norms and expectations of particular social and cultural groupings and chart their own course. For instance, an individual's rights freely to choose a marriage partner take precedence over a group's rights to maintain cultural patterns of marital preferences – even if it is argued that these norms are basic to a definition of the group's identity. As the testaments of refugees and asylum-seekers assert, many individuals have recourse only to suicide in order to avoid being forced into an unwanted marriage, and it is the responsibility of the anthropologist to support those disenfranchised individuals who find themselves under the power of others (cf. Gilad 1996). However that power is locally framed and legitimated (as that of elder kinsmen, religious experts, or whatever), here are relations of domination which anthropology should oppose. Moreover, even though the framing of these conceptions of individuals taking precedence over groups, of individual freedom *contra* cultural hegemony, derive from Western liberalism, still the United Nations International Bill of Rights which they have given rise to (comprising the Universal Declaration of Human Rights (1948), the International Covenant on Civil and Political Rights (1966), and the International Covenant on Economic, Social and Cultural Rights (1966)) is the best framework we have by which to make decisions on globally appropriate action. It suggests that 'moral imperatives know no national boundaries' (Doyal and Gough 1991: 97): it delineates that which is morally unacceptable in any socio-cultural milieu, and it proceeds towards setting universal standards of need-satisfaction and freedom of choice and movement between different forms of life.

Finally, if the discourse and law of human rights are manifestations of liberalism as a modern political philosophy, then its opposition is no less political or ideological. To decry the seeming atomism of individually-conceived human rights – in contrast, say, to notions of collective attachment, common good, public interest, patriotism, group loyalty, respect for tradition, and so on – is to extol the virtues of communitarianism: to wish to replace a politics of individual rights with a politics of common good and an emphasis on collective life and the supreme value of the community. This has long had its (equally Western) social-philosophical exponents, from Toennies and Durkheim ('[T]o experience the pleasure of saying "we", it is important not to enjoy saying "I" too much' (1973: 240)), to contemporary communitarians. However, as an ideology it can also be critiqued (cf. Phillips 1993).

As with the aforementioned illusory notions of society and culture as *sui generis*, communitarianism can be said to represent a backward-looking myth of a situation of cognitive and behavioural commonality that never existed. In practice, meanwhile, communitarianism is often hierarchical and always exclusionary with regard to those who do not belong – women and slaves, savages, pagans, Jews, Communists, homosexuals. In sociological usage, moreover, the ideology represents an attempt to 'colonize' the consciousness of individual members so that the latter are pressed into the matrices of perception of socio-cultural groupings and identify with them completely (cf. Cohen 1994). Hence, individuals come to be analytically treated as incidental to their social relationships and cultural institutions. But to ignore individual consciousness in this way, to seek simply to read it off from socio-cultural forces and forms, is to exaggerate individuals' vulnerability to these latter and underestimate their resilience. As Cohen sums up, this amounts to both flawed social science and complicity in processes of ideological hegemony. Instead, we might 'make deliberate efforts to acknowledge the subtleties, inflections and varieties of individual consciousness which are concealed by the categorical masks which we have invented so adeptly. Otherwise, we will continue to deny people the right to be themselves, deny their rights to their own identities' (Cohen 1994: 180). Self-consciousness always informs socio-cultural process and we must, as analysts, preserve individuals' rights to their own awareness and thus contribute to the decolonization of the human subject.

To say that it is impossible to consider individuals as bearers of rights independently of group memberships and identities, then, is to risk blinding oneself to those iniquitous failures of social arrangement from which liberalism has served as an escape, and to rob human beings of their best protections against abuses of power. On the other hand, to insist, as liberalism does, that the individual is the benchmark of justice, to believe the morally independent individual to be the ultimate source of value, is to direct the focus of attention to interpersonal ties not bounded groups: to 'personal communities' chosen by individuals, not ascribed ones. If community is important in people's lives, this, to repeat, must be seen to be a personal, voluntary community – of friends, neighbours, family, co-workers, co-ethnics, co-religionists – from which individuals are free to come and go. '[I]t is attachment rather than membership that is a general human value' (Phillips 1993: 194), hence, what is preferable is a political philosophy which protects the rights of attachment and detachment *per se* rather than particular (types of) attachments. Individual actors are 'the anthropological concrete' (Auge 1995: 111) and they must remain free voluntarily to adopt or reject any number of cultural personae.

This is 'post-cultural' inasmuch as it posits individuals as ontologically prior to the cultural milieux which they create and in which they dwell. It is individuals who are seen as animating, maintaining and transforming cultural truths; whatever the hegemonic community ideology concerning 'personhood' – concerning the esteeming of individualism or its negation, and the proprieties of personal public expression – a post-cultural wisdom recognizes the universal fact of individuality. It is important today for anthropologists to appreciate the right of the individual citizen to his or her own civil freedoms *against* cultural prejudices, *against* social statuses, and *against* the language embodied in their self-expressions. Human rights have a universal resonance and relevance, and their advocation is a universal responsibility. In an interdependent, post-cultural world, human rights represents a discourse offering shared standards of human dignity, and with possible procedural implications for forms of global governance.

Human rights in a post-cultural world

At the outset of *Anthropology as Cultural Critique*, Marcus and Fischer posed the provocative question: 'How is an emergent postmodern world to be represented as an object for social thought?' (1986: vii). 'Culture', as the ground for anthropological analysis, they argued, no longer remained viable in a world of global interdependence; cultural differences no longer really mattered. That is, liberal-humanist notions of general humanity now take political precedence over a highlighting of autochthonous difference, while Orientalist critique now challenges the perpetration of any form of 'othering'. Global penetrations of systems of communication and technology mean that the once distant 'exotic' informant and lay reader of anthropological texts become coevals, while the extensive movements of populations (labour migrants, refugees and tourists) make the cognitive landscapes of an increasing number of people a global one. To talk 'culture' in this setting rather than some form of 'global ecumene' could be seen, Marcus and Fischer concluded, as a romantic revelling in inessential minutiae or as an obfuscatory denial of the nature of contemporary social reality (1986: 39). It was not that the global ecumene represented a homogeneous social space, rather that difference was more that ever an internal relation: of wealth, localism, ethnicity, religiosity, sex and gender within the single social arena or polity. The question for anthropology in this post-cultural environment was both how to write the meeting of internal differences and how to right it.

Both in terms of writing this situation and of righting it, an anthropology of human rights can offer an important step forward. For, in highlighting the discourse and the laws surrounding human rights as 'transnational juridical processes' (Wilson 1997: 9) and a possible common denominator between a global diversity of individuals and groups, anthropology can advocate human rights as perhaps 'the world's first universal ideology' (Weissbrodt 1988: 1). Human rights, that is, as discourse and law, can be seen as a concrete form of Rorty's 'sacrosanct procedures' on which a global liberal polity and justice is to be founded. Here is a symbolic form in which the tensions between global and local identities may be played out – in which such differences are respected – without thereby losing sight of the ideal of reaching consensus concerning the freedom of individual practice and belief. Anthropology can show how 'human rights' can be, and is being, adopted as a resource in manifold local situations: a means by which socio-cultural identities both come together and remain distinct.

There is a flexibility in its interpretation, and yet limits are imposed beyond which violations of human rights are identifiable. As a political procedure, 'human rights' might say little substantively about the fundamentals of belief which the discourse expresses, but it does not say nothing. As Wilson spells it out (1997: 8–9), it does not countenance the maintenance of 'inegalitarian and repressive political systems', it does not entertain 'international acquiescence in state repression', and it does not place culture on the level of supreme ethical value. To the contrary, in a post-cultural world, as we have seen, the focus is firmly upon culture as optional resource, as a trope of belonging, employed by individual actors on a global stage. By writing existentialist narratives concerning human rights violations, rich in subjectivities and social relations, anthropologists can demonstrate the advantages of people the world over engaging with human rights discourses and law for the effecting and expression of a diversity of identities. They thus 'restore local subjectivities, values and memories as well as analyzing the wider global social processes in which violence is embedded' (Wilson 1997: 157).

Conclusion

Describing the need to imagine a 'post-national state' in Europe, Paul Ricoeur (1996) has suggested an appreciation of human identity as a recounted story; in a global society it is an entanglement of our own and others' stories which transpires. However, we must do more than merely share these stories, we must take responsibility for them – others' like our own. For, while it might be that the 'inalienable character of life experiences' means that we cannot directly partake of the lives of others, nevertheless, by a respectful exchange of life-narratives we can imagine our way in and we can sympathise. It is through the genuine labour of such 'narrative hospitality', for Ricoeur, that common symbolic forms might be instituted which do not replicate the closure and the structure of totalizing communities; instead, this institutionalizing would recognize the ineluctably polyglot and mobile nature of identity, in debt to the past but always in partnership with innovation. The process of reinterpretation of identity is endemic, and we must protect the conditions of its taking place.

In an anthropological dissemination of narratives of human rights, we can play our part in effecting a global society of mobile individuals who are free to believe in and practice a diversity of identities which they ongoingly create and ironically inhabit.

References

American Anthropological Association (1947) 'Statement on Human Rights', *American Anthropologist* 49,4: 539–43.

Amin, S. (1989) *L'Eurocentrisme*, Paris: Anthropos.

Ashley, K. (1990) 'Introduction', in K. Ashley (ed.) *Victor Turner and the Construction of Cultural Criticism: Between Literature and Anthropology*, Bloomington: Indiana University Press.

Auge, M. (1995) *Non-Places*, London: Verso.

Austin-Smith, B. (1990) 'Into the Heart of Irony', *Canadian Dimension* 27,7: 51–2.

Barber, B. (1996) 'Multiculturalism between Individuality and Community: Chasm or Bridge?', in A. Sarat and D. Villa (eds) *Liberal Modernism & Democratic Individuality: George Kateb and the Practice of Politics*, Princeton: Princeton University Press.

Berger, J. (1994) *A Telling Eye: The Work of John Berger*, BBC 2, 30 July.

Boulware-Miller, K. (1985) 'Female Circumcision: Challenges to the Practice as a Human Rights Violation', *Harvard Women's Law Journal* 8: 155–77.

Burridge, K. (1979) *Someone, No One. An Essay on Individuality*, Princeton: Princeton University Press.

Cohen, A. P. (1994) *Self-Consciousness: An Alternative Anthropology of Identity*, London: Routledge.

Downing, T. & Kushner, G. (eds) (1988) *Human Rights and Anthropology*, Cambridge MA: Cultural Survival.

Doyal, L. and Gough, I. (1991) *A Theory of Human Need*, Basingstoke: Macmillan.

Durkheim, E. (1973) *Moral Education*, New York: Free.

Emerson, R. W. (1981) *The Portable Emerson* (ed. C. Bode), Harmondsworth: Penguin.

Fernandez, J. (1995) 'Amazing Grace: Meaning Deficit, Displacement and New Consciousness in Expressive Interaction', in A. P. Cohen and N. Rapport (eds) *Questions of Consciousness*, London: Routledge.

Forster, E. M. (1950) *Howards End*, Harmondsworth: Penguin.

——(1972) 'What I Believe', in *Two Cheers for Democracy*, Harmondsworth: Penguin.

Gellner, E. (1993) *Postmodernism, Reason and Religion*, London: Routledge.

——(1995a) 'Anything Goes: The Carnival of Cheap Relativism which Threatens to Swamp the Coming *fin de millénaire*', *Times Literary Supplement* 4811: 6–8.

——(1995b) *Anthropology and Politics: Revolutions in the Sacred Grove*, Oxford: Blackwell.

Giddens, A. (1990) *The Consequences of Modernity*, Stanford CA: Stanford University Press.

Gilad, L. (1996) 'Cultural Collision and Human Rights', in W. Giles, H. Moussa and P. Van Esterik (eds) *Development and Diaspora: Gender and the Refugee Experience*, Dunda: Artemis.

Goody, J. (1977) *The Domestication of the Savage Mind*, Cambridge: Cambridge University Press.

Handler, R. and Segal D. (1990) *Jane Austen and the Fiction of Culture: An Essay on the Narration of Social Realities*, Tucson: University of Arizona Press.

Hutcheon, L. (1994) *Irony's Edge*, London: Routledge.

Kateb, G. (1981) 'The Moral Distinctiveness of Representative Democracy', *Ethics* 91: 357–74.

——(1984) 'Democratic Individuality and the Claim of Politics', *Political Theory* 12,3: 331–60.

——(1991) 'Democratic Individuality and the Meaning of Rights', in N. Rosenblum (ed.) *Liberalism and the Moral Life*, Cambridge MA: Harvard University Press.

Macfarlane, A. (1992) 'On Individualism', *Proceedings of the British Academy* 82: 171–199.

Marcus, G. and Fischer, M. (1986) *Anthropology as Cultural Critique*, Chicago: University of Chicago Press.

Martin, G. (1983) 'The Bridge and the River: Or The Ironies of Communication', *Poetics Today* 4,3: 415–35.

Messer, E. (1993) 'Anthropology and Human Rights', *Annual Review of Anthropology* 22: 221–49.

Nietzsche, F. (1994) *Human, All Too Human*, Harmondsworth: Penguin.

Oppenheimer, P. (1989) *The Birth of the Modern Mind: Self, Consciousness and the Invention of the Sonnet*, New York: Oxford University Press.

Ortega, J. (1956) *The Dehumanization of Art and Other Writings on Art and Culture*, New York: Doubleday.

Phillips, D. (1993) *Looking Backward: A Critical Appraisal of Communitarian Thought*, Princeton: Princeton University Press.

Rabinow, P. (1977) *Reflections on Fieldwork in Morocco*, Berkeley: University of California Press.

Rapport, N. (1993) *Diverse World-Views in an English Village*, Edinburgh: Edinburgh University Press.

——(1997) 'The 'Contrarieties' of Israel. An Essay on the Cognitive Importance and the Creative Promise of Both/And', *Journal of the Royal Anthropological Institute* 3,4: 653–72.

Ricoeur, P. (1996) *Paul Ricoeur: The Hermeneutics of Action* (ed. R. Kearney), London: Sage.

Rorty, R. (1992) *Contingency, Irony, Solidarity*, Cambridge: Cambridge University Press.

Trilling, L. (1951), *E. M. Forster*, London, Hogarth.

Weissbrodt, W. (1988) 'Human Rights: An Historical Perspective', in P. Davies (ed.) *Human Rights*, London: Routledge.

Wilson, R. (1997) 'Human Rights, Culture and Context: An Introduction', in R. Wilson (ed.) *Human Rights, Culture and Context: Anthropological Perspectives*, London: Pluto.

Chapter 9

Epilogue

Anthony P. Cohen

As the editor of this volume, Vered Amit has taken on the formidable task of producing a current account of one of the classical concepts in the social sciences, 'community', formidable not only because the concept has changed substantially over the decades in which the literature has accumulated, but because much of the literature has been concerned with its slipperiness as a concept. Community has never been a term of lexical precision, though much tedious work has been dedicated to the fruitless effort to so render it. The literature, unsurprisingly, has tracked the paradigmatic shifts of sociocultural anthropology and sociology; and perhaps what makes our present editor's task so difficult is that we are writing at a moment when no paradigm dominates, indeed when the very notion of a paradigm has come to seem rather unfashionable. The authors of this book have therefore completed an interesting and exemplary circle. Half a century ago, anthropologists and sociologists took the word 'community' (and so many others) from ordinary language and tried to transform it into an analytical category with scientific rigour. Our present authors are returning it whence it came, having decided (entirely justifiably, in my view) that there is no mileage in trying to define it, and are describing its ordinary popular use. It is an exercise entirely appropriate to the ethnographic and anthropological enterprise.

Because it has been quite frequently cited in this volume of essays, and would appear to have had some influence on writers over the years, I should say something for the record about *The Symbolic Construction of Community* (Cohen 1985). Authors know well that years after they wrote the work in question, people tend to refer to the views expressed in it as if they were somehow timeless, implying that they have not changed during the period which has since elapsed. The fact that readers reconstruct writers' ideas and theories, and then attribute to them opinions which they have never held or never expressed is an occupational hazard for which writers themselves must take much of the blame: perhaps if they wrote with more clarity and precision, they would be less vulnerable to misrepresentation and misinterpretation. My concern here is not that I have had attributed to me views which I do not hold; but to explain that I had come to feel very uncertain about much of what I argued in the book even before it was published.

I wrote *The Symbolic Construction of Community* in six months, although I had been thinking about it for many years, and had annually given a course of lectures, which provided the basis of the book, for seven or eight years previously. The book was written, somewhat reluctantly, to a commission: I was heartily tired of the topic, having been rehearsing it to students over so many years, and doubted whether I had anything novel or useful left to say. However, I was housebound for the best part of a year while convalescing from major surgery, and I decided to write the book both to fulfil a contractual obligation, and to get myself back to work and back into writing mode. The writing was a chore, and I completed it with an enormous sense of relief that I had finally acquitted myself of a wearisome commitment, and with the expectation that the book would rapidly drop out of sight.

To my great and genuine surprise, this was not to be. I have never wavered from my view that it is the least meritorious of the four books I have written. To my chagrin, it has outsold the other three books put together, has never been out of print, and has sold into the tens of thousands all over the world. Immediately following its publication, it won a *CHOICE* award; has been the subject of postgraduate theses in North America and Australia, and continues to be referred to with tedious frequency. The displeasure I express here about the book is not false modesty. It was written against prior paradigms; but, of course, was itself paradigm-bound. The fact is that by the time I had sent the typescript off to the publisher, I was already in fundamental disagreement with one of its central arguments from which I have been distancing myself ever since. The argument was precisely the one with which Signe Howell and John Gray take issue in this volume: the attribution to identity of the characteristics of relativity and an ephemeral nature; and concomitantly, the denial to identity (communal or individual) of constancy. My reaction against this position was motivated less by a critique of the literature on community as such than it was against the idea of boundary and identity expounded in Barth's classic 1969 essay, and reiterated subsequently by countless authors in innumerable publications. I later went on to argue emphatically and excessively against (a) the relativism of the boundary-focused thesis (a position which, in turn, I have had recently to qualify

(Cohen 2000)); and (b) against the neglect of the community's self-identity which, like the individual's, is likely, in part, to be non-relativistic and non-contingent, the same argument which John Gray makes in this volume, and which was the subject of my 1994 book, *Self Consciousness*.

I have no wish to disown *The Symbolic Construction of Community*. I advocated its ideas once, but I do not feel under any obligation to defend them for ever. I have wondered about its apparent and continuing popularity – a Turkish translation has just appeared – and have never supposed it was due to the intellectual brilliance of the author. Obviously, it was timely, perhaps for two reasons. The first was that, as well as challenging both old approaches to community and critiques of them, it coincided and was consistent with attempts by a variety of scholars to move away from the old analogic approach to the interpretation of symbolism. This was and is a matter principally for anthropologists, and I need not pursue it here, not least because 'symbol' and cognate concepts have been picked up and employed by other social scientists in these later uses, and the earlier arguments are largely irrelevant to them.

Second, at the time when I began to formulate them, in the early 1970s, the theoretical literature on community, such as it was, had become appallingly arid, turning endlessly on problems of definition and, even more speciously, of valorization. The latter has simply disappeared with the effective demise of Marxist critiques in anthropology and sociology. The former has passed, like so many of our problems, out of the scholarly realm into that of ordinary language. Walking recently through the nature reserve near my home in Edinburgh, I came upon a newly fenced enclosure. Pinned to the fence was a notice announcing: 'Fragile plant community'. The middle-aged pedant in me thinks, '"Fragile plant community", indeed! What have we come to?' But people are much less bothered now about the accurate or correct use of language than they were during my education and apprenticeship. Wittgenstein's admonition to attend to use rather than to lexical meaning seems popularly to have come of age. I do not defend this state of affairs, but merely acknowledge that this is the way it seems to be. 'Community' is used so variously, even inconsistently, and so loosely that, paradigm considerations apart, it has ceased to be of any obvious analytical use as a category in social science. It indicates collectivity or communality or even just similarity of a sort, but these can be at any level from the global to the local. As is apparent from the essays here, the condition which is supposedly shared among individuals, such that they are designated as 'a community', may not entail consciousness of the fact, and certainly does not seem to require that the condition of community extends beyond the specific item which people are presumed to share. Communities, in Amit's nice phrase, may be 'without place'.[1] In the cases reported here, they are adoptive parents who may not know each other; they are relatives who bear the burdens of supporting their athletic kin; they are farmers who apparently adhere to strong views about a certain breed of sheep (though personally I am sceptical about this); they are populations related ethnically and/or religiously in ways which distinguish them from their near-neighbours. Sometimes 'community' is used synonymously with 'society'; sometimes it seems to be used to suggest a discrimination between 'us' (those who abide by rules/laws/conventions) as opposed to 'them', those who do not; sometimes it is employed in a way which does not convey any meaning at all ('the community of nations'; 'fragile plant community').

It seems really quite pointless to bemoan the absence of precision, since we live for better or worse in a post-modern demotic age, in which the depredations of tabloid journalism, and the semantic abuses perpetrated by politicians and the media are more authoritative than *Fowler's Correct Usage*. There is no generally acknowledged or accepted theory of community, but there never was. But if it doesn't mean anything in particular, as would appear to be the case, how can the word have any analytic or descriptive value? And if it lacks any such value, what is the justification for gathering together into one volume a set of essays which do not share a common referent?

The point is, of course, that Vered Amit and her contributors are writing about the sentiments of community which are of our age; and which, arguably, are more sensitive to reality than were those sociologists of thirty, forty or fifty years ago who were more concerned with semantic discriminations. People are associated with each other now only for limited purposes or in limited respects. Farmers in the Scottish Borders *may* agree with each other about sheep; but this does not entail that they share political views, or religious beliefs, or similar opinions about the residents of neighbouring Borders towns, or that they agree with each other about whether women should be allowed to ride in the Common Ridings. The adoptive parents about whom Signe Howell writes have the special nature of their parenthood in common, but possibly nothing else. The parents who are Noel Dyck's concern probably differ from each other in countless respects. But this variety, the lack of homogeneity, is in the character of contemporary Western life. In Rapport's view, it is even more fundamental and general: that it is the nature of individuals that they differ from each other: they use their 'shared' culture to express both their similarities to and divergences from each other; they use their capacity for irony as individuals to connect fact to value through the medium of community-derived means of expression. Individuals *qua* members of a community are thus, in Vered Amit's wonderful phrase,[2] 'stakeholders in a cultural inventory'; but their stakes differ, as do their perceptions of the inventory itself.

'Community', then, has become a way of designating that *some*thing is shared among a group of people at a time when we no longer assume that *anything* is necessarily shared. This is not a trivial matter. One might expect that sentiments of 'community' are simply anachronistic in the age of globalism, as people *communi*cate across the ether, crossing political and geographical boundaries both virtually and physically, and as mobility and migration makes for increasingly heterogeneous societies. Yet, notwithstanding its imprecision, community seems to have remained a compelling idea, perhaps indicating a yearning for a degree of commonality and for a focus on those social features which conjoin people rather than those which divide them. As a renascent liberalism came to dominate Western polities during the late 1990s, it briefly spawned its own social theory, 'Communitarianism' (a specious sociological gloss on The Third Way), a set of largely vacuous postulates which promptly wilted under critical scrutiny and analysis. 'Community' now seems to have become a normative rather than a descriptive term, and perhaps that is appropriate to contemporary urban Western societies.

Or perhaps communities *are* just as prevalent now as we supposed them to be in previous times and other social circumstances, but we are failing to see them, because they take different forms or are more covert. There is anyway a danger in confusing an analytic category with an approximation. Even used descriptively across and within different societies to denote groups of people who live 'with' or close to each other, 'community' is so vague as to be virtually meaningless. It doesn't follow that we should ban it from use – only that it is futile to try to theorize community other than in its *particular* uses. As a term deployed indigenously, say by Dawson's Ashington miners, we have something to work on ethnographically and interpretively. Simply to indicate, what Karen Fog Olwig neatly calls, 'fields of shared belonging', there is nothing much we can do with the word: the important tasks being rather to identify the field and its extent, and the significance to it of what it is that is deemed to be shared. We do need to beware of falling into an atavistic trap of supposing communities to have existed once, but now to have been superseded by social change. The most we should allow here is that communities may now differ from their prior forms – nothing very startling about that – and that the nature of people's belonging to the various communities with which they identify may also have changed. The essays in this volume are eloquent testimony to that. But let's not waste time and energy on semantic neuroses and anxiety about the word.

Anderson's suggestion in 1983 that communities should be thought of as imagined entities, and mine in 1985 that they are symbolic constructs, did not deny the reality of communities. They were just attempts to capture what it is that people use the word to signify. I think the very disparate cases reported here sustain those approaches. My discomfort has been with the relativism and contingency that I previously read into the construct, but certainly not with the notional character of community as a concept. I don't see this as a distinctively post-modern or post-structural or post-anything reading of community. It is simply a stab at what people seem to have meant, and to continue to mean when they use the word. The referents of the word may have changed, no longer necessarily expressing locality or spatial contiguity, but the sense has not. This afterword to Vered Amit's present exploration of the subject is, hopefully, my last word on it.

Notes

1 This refers to the original unpublished proposal for this volume, drafted by Vered Amit
2 Unpublished proposal, Amit, n.d.

References

Anderson, Benedict (1983/1991) *Imagined Communities: Reflections on the Origin and Spread of Nationalism*. London and New York: Verso.

Barth, Fredrik (1969) 'Introduction' to F. Barth (ed.) *Ethnic Groups and Boundaries*, pp. 9–38. London: George Allen & Unwin.

Cohen, Anthony P. (1985) *The Symbolic Construction of Community*. London and New York: Tavistock Publications.

Cohen, Anthony P. (1994) *Self Consciousness: An Alternative Anthropology of Identity*. London: Routledge.

Cohen, Anthony P. (ed.) (2000) *Signifying Identities: Anthropological Perspectives on Boundaries and Contested Values*. London and New York: Routledge.

Index